Assaye 1803

Wellington's first and 'bloodiest' victory

Campaign • 166

Assaye 1803

Wellington's first and 'bloodiest' victory

Simon Millar • Illustrated by Peter Dennis

First published in Great Britain in 2006 by Osprey Publishing,
Midland House, West Way, Botley, Oxford OX2 0PH, UK
44-02 23rd St, Suite 219, Long Island City, NY 11101, USA
Email: info@ospreypublishing.com

Transferred to digital print on demand 2010

First published 2006
1st impression 2006

Printed and bound in Great Britain

A CIP catalogue record for this book is available from the British Library

ISBN: 978 1 84603 001 7

Design by Black Spot
Index by Alison Worthington
Cartography by The Map Studio
3D bird's-eye view by Black Spot
Originated by PPS Grasmere Ltd, Leeds, UK

Dedication
To the officers and men of the old East India Company Army; and Rupert.

Acknowledgements
I have received considerable assistance in writing this book and must thank:
Lt Col Pradeep Bhatia Indian Army, David Rowlands, Lt Col Sharnapa
Indian Army, Lt Col (Retd) Cumming RHQ The Highlanders, Major (Retd)
John Conway of the SASC Museum in Warminster, Peter Harrington
of the Anne S.K. Brown University Library (ASKB), Martin Mintz and
Sandra Powlette of the British Library (BL), Jessica Talmage of the
Mary Evans Picture Library (MEPL), Kirbie Crowe of the Bridgeman
Art Library (BAL) and Helen Dobson of the Victoria & Albert Museum
(VAM). My thanks also go to Nikolai Bogdanovic for his support and
Peter Dennis, for turning my ideas into great pictures.

The Woodland Trust
Osprey Publishing is supporting the Woodland Trust, the UK's leading
woodland conservation charity, by funding the dedication of trees.

www.ospreypublishing.com

Artist's note
Readers may care to note the original paintings from which the colour
plates in this book were prepared are available for private sale.
All reproduction copyright whatsoever is retained by the publisher.
Enquiries should be addressed to:

Peter Dennis
Fieldhead
The Park
Mansfield
Nottinghamshire
NG18 2AT
UK

The publishers regret that they can enter into no correspondence upon
this matter.

Glossary of terms
Distances, ranges, and dimensions are given in inches, feet, yards, and
statute miles rather than metric:

feet to metres:	multiply feet by 0.31
yards to metres:	multiply yards by 0.91
miles to kilometres:	multiply miles by 1.61

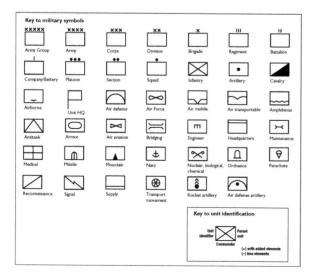

CONTENTS

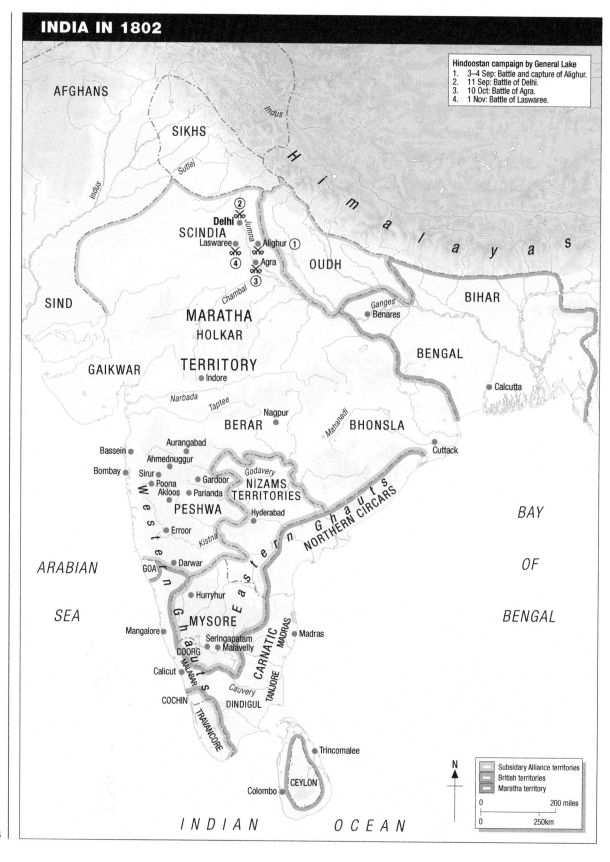

INDIA IN 1802

Hindoostan campaign by General Lake
1. 3–4 Sep: Battle and capture of Alighur.
2. 11 Sep: Battle of Delhi.
3. 10 Oct: Battle of Agra.
4. 1 Nov: Battle of Laswaree.

AFGHANS

SIKHS

Indus

Sutlej

Indus

H i m a l a y a s

SCINDIA

② Delhi
Jumna
Laswaree ● ● Alighur ①
④ ● Agra
③

SIND

OUDH

MARATHA

HOLKAR

Chambal

Ganges
Benares ●

BIHAR

GAIKWAR

TERRITORY

● Indore

BENGAL

Narbada *Taptee*

● Nagpur

BERAR

Mahanadi

BHONSLA

● Calcutta

Bassein ●
Aurangabad ●
Ahmednuggur ●
Bombay ● Sirur ●
● Poona ● Gardoor
Akloos ● ● Parianda

Godavery

NIZAMS
TERRITORIES

Cuttack ●

PESHWA
Erroor ●

Hyderabad ●

Kistna

E
a
s
t
e
r
n

G h a u t s

NORTHERN CIRCARS

GOA ● Darwar

● Hurryhur

W
e
s
t
e
r
n

G
h
a
t
s

BAY

OF

ARABIAN

SEA

MYSORE

Mangalore ●
Seringapatam ●
● Malavelly

CARNATIC

MADRAS

● Madras

BENGAL

COORG

Calicut ●

MALABAR

TANJORE

COCHIN
DINDIGUL

Cauvery

TRAVANCORE

● Trincomalee

N

Subsidary Alliance territories
British territories
Maratha territory

CEYLON

Colombo ●

0   200 miles

0   250km

I N D I A N   O C E A N

6

THE ORIGINS OF THE CAMPAIGN

The central southern part of India, particularly the tableland between the eastern and western Ghauts, is known as the Deccan. In this highland, the dust settles easily on the leaves of the banyan trees, even after a burst of monsoon rainfall. It is August 1803 and Major-General Arthur Wellesley watches the column of red-coated soldiers as they march through a countryside of scattered farmsteads, fallow fields and those of cereal crops and onions, with the occasional shade from a mango tree providing a brief relief from the heat of the day. He nods his head in approval, beckons to his small band of staff officers to follow him as he urges his horse into a walk and turns to ride towards the head of the column.

Wellesley was one of two brothers who had both made the long sea journey to 'Hindustan' in the last few years of the 18th century, and who were both to have a huge impact in the coming years. On each occasion as their ship anchored in the Hoogly River, next to Fort William and Calcutta, they had stood on deck taking in the initial sights, sounds and smells of India which emanated from the green shore. Arthur Wellesley had been the first to arrive in February 1797 at the age of 28. He was a young colonel commanding his regiment, the 33rd Foot, with his experience of war limited to the Duke of York's debacle in the 1794–95 campaign in the Netherlands. In April 1798 his elder brother, Richard Colley Wellesley, second Earl of Mornington, arrived to take up his post as governor general, in succession to Sir John Shore. Mornington was to be responsible for the three British presidencies of Calcutta, Madras and

The esplanade at Calcutta with ships anchored on the Hoogly. This is the scene that would have greeted both of the Wellesley brothers. Fort William is on the right. (British Library)

A European gentleman with his *moonshee* or 'native professor' of languages. Many Europeans took pride in learning the native languages of India. (Author's collection)

A gentleman delivering a letter to a *soon-tah-burdar*, or 'silver baton bearer'. These servants were retained by persons of rank by carrying messages they were also the eyes and ears of a commander, and were *hircarrahs* of a sort. The message was carried in the baton. (Author's collection)

Bombay. In the relatively short time he was to be in India, Mornington was to have a profound effect on Indian affairs and the projection of British influence and power.

The post of governor general had been created as a result of the India Act of 1784, introduced by William Pitt, which sought to bring under government control British policy in the east. The act created a Board of Control appointed by the king, consisting of ministers who would be responsible for 'the superintendence and control over all the British territorial possessions in the East Indies and over affairs of the [East India] Company'.

The British possessions of the East India Company were based on the presidency towns of Calcutta, Madras and Bombay. The Calcutta Presidency consisted of the provinces of Bengal, Bihar, a part of Orissa, and Chittagong on the far side of the Bay of Bengal. The only additions to the territory since Lord Clive's time had been Warren Hastings' acceptance of the suzerainty over Benares and Ghazipur in 1775. The fortress of Allahabad was taken over from the Nawab of Oudh in the time of Sir John Shore. The 1782 Treaty of Salbye had stripped Governor Duncan (Bombay) of territory occupied during the first Anglo-Maratha War (1775–76 and 1779–82) leaving Bombay to consist of two islands: Bombay and Salsette. Madras, the oldest of the three presidencies, was made up of various territories, each of a different tenure. The Company possessed the presidency town of Madras with some adjoining villages and three districts gained as a result of the Treaty of Seringapatam with Tippu Sultan in 1793.

Calcutta alone controlled a hinterland large enough to raise sufficient revenue to support the East India Company armies in all their Indian possessions. The India Act granted supremacy to Bengal, yet all three presidencies were, to a great measure, self-contained and independent; this was reflected in the fact that although relations between them were harmonious, it was in the form of friendly states rather than as sister provincial governments answering to a superior authority.

We must now look at the Indian 'country' powers (independent states) which, on Mornington's arrival, the East India Company needed to find a policy towards. To the north-west of Bengal lay the populous land of Oudh, still nominally independent but controlled by the British Resident. The reigning Nawab, Saadat Ali, was not popular and in 1797 his throne seemed far from secure. What remained of the Mughal Empire was ruled by the Mughal Emperor, Shah Alam, whose power was a shadow of its former self. Shah Alam had had to rely on the Marathas to restore him to his throne in 1771, and he continued to rely on them for protection. This is illustrated by the capture of Shah Alam in 1788 by an Afghan chief who blinded him, when deprived of Maratha protection for just a few months. Further to the north-west again were the Sikhs, of whom little was known at the time, other than they were not expected to be able to check an expected invasion of the plains of India by Zeman Shah, the ruler of Afghanistan, when in 1796 the Afghans appeared at Lahore. In the south the Nawab of Arcot was so heavily in debt to the Company that he was hardly regarded as independent. The Nizam of Hyderabad was nominally the overlord of the Deccan and had been an ally of the British. His loyalty however was alienated when Sir John Shore refused to support him against the Marathas in 1795. He was defeated at the Battle of Kharda and although he managed, in effect, to escape from the terms imposed upon him by the Marathas, he was still overshadowed by their influence. His chief support, apart from the Marathas, was his 14,000-man army, trained and commanded by French officers. British influence over the Deccan therefore looked destined to pass into the hands of either their great European rival or the largest of the country powers. To the south-west of Hyderabad was the ancient Hindu state of Mysore. The sullen and vengeful Tippu had lost half of his territory after his defeat at the hands of Cornwallis during the Third Anglo-Mysore War of 1789–92, and had allied himself with Revolutionary France for the purpose of attacking British India. The final country power, and the most dominant and formidable, was that of the Marathas. The Marathas were a loose confederation of states controlling a great tract of land stretching across central India, whose rulers were Scindia of Gwalior, Holkar of Indore, the Raja of Berar, the Gaikwar of Baroda, and their nominal head the Raja of Satara. The Rajas of Satara, however, had been usurped by their chief minister, the Peshwa, and it was the Peshwa who was the power within the confederacy.

Mornington, within a short time of arriving in India, set himself the task of altering the political structure of the country powers. His plan was to create a series of subsidiary alliances, which would place the East India Company in a dominant position in India. The subsidiary alliance was when a country power, in return for a defensive guarantee, would have British troops stationed in their territory, subsidized by themselves. The protected state in effect lost its right to an independent foreign policy and British paramountcy would be achieved.

A palanquin. This was a favoured mode of transport by many Europeans. Some officers even had their palanquin bearers on campaign with them. (Author's collection)

THE TIGER OF MYSORE

Tippu Sultan was the first problem to confront Mornington. The Treaty of Seringapatam in 1793 had deprived Tippu of nearly half his lands, and nursing his grievances he turned to the French to help recover them. He had little or no knowledge of the true state of affairs in Europe, the difficulty for the French in carrying out a war in India, or of giving him any tangible help at all. The small contingent of Frenchmen at his court, no better informed, told him exaggerated success stories of French Revolutionary arms in Europe and of the ability of France to support him against the British. Governor Malaric of Mauritius, on receiving a deputation from Tippu, publicly proclaimed an alliance between the French Republic and Mysore. With Tippu planting the tree of liberty at Seringapatam, being elected to the Jacobin Club, and a handful of French troops landing at Mangalore, Mornington determined on war.

Operations against Tippu had to be postponed for a year because of the unprepared state of the military forces at Madras. During this time Mornington tried to revive the tripartite treaty of 1790 with the Marathas and Hyderabad. The Marathas kept aloof, but Hyderabad he bound to the British cause by the first use of the subsidiary alliance clause that implied the subordination of the Nizam to the British government in matters of foreign policy and external relations; the maintenance and payment of a contingent of Company troops; and the expulsion of

Government House, Calcutta. This was Mornington's residence as governor general. Fort William is behind and the masts of ships anchored on the Hoogly can just be seen. (British Library)

The Battle of Malavelly, March 27, 1799. This was the first encounter between Tippu and General Harris. Tippu was defeated and withdrew to Seringapatam. (Author's collection)

officers of other European nations. The Madras government was typically feeble, but Mornington bore down on their opposition and the disbandment of the Nizam's French-trained and officered force was carried out with great adroitness by the Resident, James Achilles Kirkpatrick. At the same time an intercepted letter from Bonaparte at Cairo to Tippu proved that the action had been taken not a moment too soon. Mornington had decided back in June how he was going to deal with Tippu and he played his diplomatic game with consummate skill. In November 1798 and again in January 1799 Mornington sent letters informing Tippu of Bonaparte's landing in Egypt, the British victory at the Battle of the Nile, and his knowledge of Tippu's intrigues with the French; furthermore, he demanded absolute submission from him. Tippu's dilatory reaction to the letters and evasive responses were swept aside by Mornington. By the time Tippu realized the British were in earnest it was too late. Two armies were converging upon his capital.

The main army commanded by General Harris, in conjunction with the Nizam's army, nominally commanded by Mir Allam but in reality commanded by Colonel Arthur Wellesley, set off from Vellore on February 11 in the east and entered Mysore on March 5. The second (Bombay) army was commanded by General Stuart and advanced from Cannanore on February 21, via the Western Ghauts. Tippu struck at both the western and eastern invasions. His first attack was on Stuart's force at Sedaseer, some 45 miles from the capital, on March 6, where he was defeated with a loss of 1,500 men. Turning eastwards he marched to face Harris and on March 27 at Malavelly, 30 miles east of Seringapatam, he was defeated again. Tippu now had no option but to withdraw to his capital. Tippu expected the attack on the city to come from the north, but Harris crossed the Cauvery River at Sosilay and attacked from the south-west. A panicked Tippu attempted to negotiate, but baulked at the conditions, saying that 'it was better to die like a soldier than live a miserable dependent on the infidels'.

Seringapatam was stormed on May 4 and amid fierce fighting the British lost 1,164 men and the defenders close on 8,000. Tippu died fighting in the breach. The campaign had been a brilliant success.

'THE MOST SALUTARY AND USEFUL MEASURES'

In October 1799 a subsidiary treaty was made with the Raja of Tanjore, and in Surat Mornington took advantage of a change in succession to pension off the Nawab and assume complete control. The Nawab of Arcot was next to be dealt with. The administration of the Carnatic had long been an open scandal; the dual government had dishonoured the Nawab and so

The storming of Seringapatam, May 4, 1799. The capture of Seringapatam and the death of Tippu Sahib ended Muslim dominance over Hindu Mysore. (Bridgeman Art Library)

Fort St George, Madras. Madras was on the Coromandel Coast of India. There was no harbour and so surf boats were used to take passengers ashore – and not without the occasional fatality. (Author's collection)

The West Gate of Fort St George, Madras. Madras was the headquarters for British affairs in southern India. (Bridgeman Art Library)

corrupted the civil servants in Madras that the Presidency possessed the worst reputation. Under the treaty made with Cornwallis the British were empowered in time of war to assume total control of the administration; in capturing Seringapatam, evidence was found that the Nawab and his son had entered into correspondence with Tippu. Mornington did not immediately invoke the treaty, but in 1801 when the Nawab died, he did so and the British assumed control of the Carnatic government. Mornington's attention was now directed to his northern frontier, where in the buffer state of Oudh he saw a weak defence on the north-western boundary of Bengal. Mornington called upon the Nawab to disband a portion of his own largely ineffective army and receive a larger subsidiary force; the Nawab at first resisted, but tiring of Mornington's continual pressure he offered to abdicate. This was eagerly welcomed by the Governor General, but the Nawab had only contemplated it on the condition that his son succeeded him; when Mornington baulked at this stipulation, the offer was withdrawn. A new draft subsidiary treaty was presented to the Nawab, who protested with some ability but was ignored by Mornington. In the end the Nawab submissively gave way. As part of the

Big cat hunting. Hunting was a favourite pastime for natives and Europeans in India. This was a dangerous sport, as leopards were known to leap out of trees at the hunter. (Private collection)

treaty Mornington had demanded the territory of Rohilkhand and the land between the Ganges and Jumna rivers. Oudh was now surrounded by British territory that abutted the Himalayas and followed the ill-defined boundary of the Marathas' (Scindia's) dominions in northern India.

The Marathas presented Mornington with his final obstacle. The revised subsidiary treaty with the Nizam of Hyderabad, where the East India Company engaged to protect his ill-defined territories against all enemies, was viewed by the Marathas with great uneasiness. They had a considerable fear of this thrusting of British influence into their own territories and the loss of a fertile plundering ground. However, as long as they remained united they would have little to fear; British statesmen dreaded antagonizing this resolute race of warriors. Their own internal dissention, however, would be their nemesis, and the seed of this was sown with the death of Nana Farnavis in Poona, in March 1800. Nana Farnavis was a shrewd statesman and with him, in the words of the British Resident, 'departed all the wisdom and moderation of the Maratha government'. At once, both Daulat Rao Scindia (of Gwalior) and Jaswant Rao Holkar (of Indore) vied for the upper hand at Poona. Of the two, Holkar was the stronger and most enterprizing of the Maratha princes, but the dithering Peshwa, Baji Rao II, submitted to the control of Scindia. On October 23, 1802 Holkar defeated the combined armies of the Peshwa and Scindia outside Poona.

The Peshwa initially took refuge in a hill fort in Konton and then made for the coast. In due course, after several changes of residence, he arrived in Bassein in the East India Company ship *Herculean*. The policy of Mornington's predecessors would have been to let the Marathas sort out their disputes on their own, whilst protecting the border of Hyderabad. Mornington, however, believed that a policy of non-intervention was putting off the evil day and foresaw the danger of the Peshwa, if rebuffed in his appeals for help, throwing himself on the French for support as the Nizam had done in 1795. So the British agreed to restore the Peshwa to his throne.

CHRONOLOGY

1796

April	33rd Foot embark and sail to India.
3 May	Arthur Wellesley promoted to colonel.
September	Wellesley joins the 33rd Foot at the Cape of Good Hope.

1797

February	Wellesley and the 33rd Foot arrive at Fort William (Calcutta).
August	Wellesley and 33rd Foot part of expedition to Penang. The Earl of Mornington (Richard Wellesley) succeeds as governor general.
November	Arthur Wellesley and 33rd Foot back at Calcutta.
November 9	Mornington sails for India.

1798

January–March	Arthur Wellesley in Madras.
January	Mysorean envoys arrive at Port Louis, Mauritius.
April	French 'contingent' arrives at Mangalore, Mysore.
May 17	Mornington arrives at Fort William.
May 19	Bonaparte sails for Egypt.
July 21	French defeat Mameluks at Battle of Pyramids.
July 24	French enter Cairo.
August 1–2	Battle of the Nile. French fleet destroyed.
September	33rd Foot placed on Madras establishment.
September 1	First subsidiary alliance with Nizam of Hyderabad.
November	Mornington's first letter to Tippu.
December	Bonaparte learns of Tippu's actions against British.
December 18	Arthur Wellesley appointed to command forces concentrating at Arcot, Arnee, and Vellore.
December 25	Mornington receives Tippu's prevaricating response.

1799

January	Mornington's second letter to Tippu. Wellesley relinquishes command to General Harris.
February	Wellesley appointed to command Hyderabad subsidiary force.
February 11	Harris begins the advance on Seringapatam.
February 21	General Stuart marches on Seringapatam from Cannanore.
March 6	Battle of Sedaseer, Stuart defeats Tippu.
March 27	Battle of Malavelly, Harris defeats Tippu.
April 3	British arrive outside Seringapatam.
May 4	Storming and capture of Seringapatam.
May 5	Wellesley appointed to command the city.
July 9	Wellesley appointed Governor of Seringapatam.
September 11	Wellesley appointed to command all Mysore.

1800

| March | Nana Farnavis, Maratha statesman, dies in Poona. |
| June 24 | Campaign against Doondiah Waugh begins. |

September 10	Battle of Conaghull. Doondiah defeated and killed.
October	Wellesley sent to Ceylon to command expeditionary force gathering at Trincomalee.
November 15	Wellesley appointed to command the force gathering at Trincomalee.

1801

January	Mornington appoints General Baird to command at Trincomalee.
February 11	Expedition sails for the Red Sea.
February 15	Wellesley sails for Bombay.
March	Wellesley ill with the 'Malabar itch'.
March 21	Battle of Alexandria. British under Abercromby defeat French under Menou.
April 28	Wellesley returns to Seringapatam and resumes command of Mysore.
August 30	Menou surrenders to the British in Egypt.
September 14	French expedition to Egypt ends; French embark for France.
November 10	Subsidiary alliance treaty with the Nawab of Oudh signed.

1802

January/February	Operations against the Raja of Bellum.
March 25	Peace of Amiens.
April	Wellesley promoted to major-general.
September 6	Wellesley receives news of his promotion.
October 23	Battle of Poona. Holkar defeats the combined forces of Scindia and the Peshwa.
November 12	Wellesley receives orders to command army forming on the Tombuddra.
December 31	Treaty of Bassein signed.

1803

February 27	Wellesley appointed to command the army to restore the Peshwa assembled at Hurryhur.
March 9	Wellesley advances from Hurryhur.
April 20	Wellesley arrives in Poona.
May 13	Restoration of the Peshwa.
June 26	Wellesley appointed to command political and military affairs in the Deccan.
July	Operations in Hindustan. General Lake's headquarters at Cawnpore.
August 6	Maratha War commences.
August 7	Hindustan: Lake marches up the Ganges to Kanoge.
August 8	British troops storm the *pettah* of Ahmednugger.
August 12	The fort of Ahmednugger surrenders.
August 12–September 20	Wellesley marches against the combined Maratha forces of Scindia and Berar.
August 29–September 4	Hindustan: siege and capture of Aligarth.
September 11	Hindustan: Battle of Delhi.
September 21	Wellesley and Stevenson in conference about the campaign.
September 23	Battle of Assaye.
October 16	Stevenson captures Burhampoor.
October 24	The fortress of Asseerghur capitulates to Stevenson.
November 1	Battle of Laswaree.
November 13–December 26	Hindustan: Lake's operations about Deig.
November 29	The Battle of Argaum. Wellesley and Stevenson combined defeat Marathas.
December 15	The fortress of Gwalighur taken by storm.
December 17	Treaty of Deogum with Bhonsla Raja of Berar.
December 30	Treaty with Daulat Rao Scindia, Raja of Gwalior.

OPPOSING COMMANDERS

THE MARATHAS

The Marathas are a Hindu people, and their most famous ruler was Shivaji, who in 1674 carved out an independent Maratha domain around Poona from the Bijapur Sultanate. This land became known as the Maratha Empire or Confederacy. In 1680, after a lifetime of guerilla warfare with the Mughal Emperor Aurangzeb, Shivaji died leaving a great Maratha kingdom in central India, but with ill-defined boundaries. Aurangzeb's death in 1707 not only ended a period of great instability, but also Muslim dominance in India. The descendants of Shivaji continued to rule, but not without internal discord, throughout the 18th century. During this period, the power of the office of the Peshwa (chief minister) had become so great that they became the dispensers of Maratha power and patronage. Baji Rao I (Peshwa 1720–40), possibly the greatest of the Peshwas, distributed the ceded Deccan revenues amongst the various Maratha commanders, which in turn produced a common interest. His exceptional talents also ensured there was firm leadership. The Maratha confederacy was divided amongst the Gaekwads of Baroda, Holkars of Indore and Malwa, and the Scindias of Gwalior; these Maratha Maharajas were the strongholds of Maratha power. The last Peshwa was Baji Rao II, who after the Battle of Poona (October 1802) sought refuge with the British and signed the Treaty of Bassein. His last act as Peshwa was to lead the Maratha Confederacy to defeat in the Third Anglo-Maratha War of 1817–18, which left the British in control of most of India. The Maratha heartland of Desh, including Poona, came under direct British rule; while the states of Gwalior, Indore, and Nagpur were integrated into the British Raj as princely states that retained local autonomy. This great empire is today preserved in the Indian state of Maharashtra.

Daulat Rao Scindia, Maharaja of Gwalior (1779–1827) succeeded his great uncle and adopted father, Mahadji Rao Scindia, on February 12, 1794. He inherited from Mahadji Rao an army well equipped and exceptionally well trained by the Savoyard adventurer Benoit de Boigne. His European-officered *compoos* (roughly a brigade in size) led by Pohlmann in the Deccan and by Perron in Hindustan were the mainstay of the Maratha army.

Colonel Pohlmann, a Hanoverian by birth, had come out to India when in a Hanoverian regiment and was quartered in Madras. He entered de Boigne's service in 1792 or 1793 and by 1794 was a captain. By 1795 he was in command of a battalion in the Second Brigade at Mattra, which also saw the service of James Skinner. Between 1795 and 1799 Pohlmann gained much experience and in early 1799 Perron, who had taken over from De Boigne as the overall commander of Scindia's troops, began to distrust Sutherland who commanded the Second

Baji Rao II, Peshwa of the Marathas. He was an able administrator, but was susceptible to being easily swayed by more dominant personalities. He eventually led the Marathas to their complete defeat at British hands in the war of 1817–19. (Author's collection)

Brigade, removing and replacing him with Pohlmann. At Assaye he effectively commanded all the regular battalions in the Maratha army, after Scindia and Berar absented themselves before the start of the battle. His well-drilled battalions were easily a match for native Indian opponents, but at Assaye where they faced a British force of European and Sepoy battalions for the first time, they gave way, and fell into some disorder after the battle. Herbert Compton describes him as 'a cheerful and entertaining character who lived in the style of an Indian prince, kept a seraglio, and always travelled on an elephant, attended by a guard of Mughals, all dressed alike in purple robes'.

There were many **European officers** in the service of the Marathas in the late 1790s and early 1800s. Many were British and left Maratha service as a result of not wanting to take up arms against their fellow countrymen; James Skinner and William Gardner were such men. Two more of these officers in the pay were at Assaye. Colonel Saleur, a Swiss-born officer who commanded the forces of the Begum Somru, marched in 1802 with five battalions to join Scindia in the Deccan, and when war broke out with the British he was still with Scindia. All the battalions were at Assaye, but only one actually took part in the fighting, the other four having been left behind to guard the baggage and as a result escaped destruction. Major John James Dupont was a Dutchman by birth and commanded one of Scindia's *compoos* of four battalions at Assaye and shared in the defeat and dispersion of the Maratha army.

The elephant of a prince or general. Elephants were commonly used by native princes and generals as platforms from which to command. Colonel Pohlmann was said to have commanded at Assaye from one of his elephants. (Engraving after Stanley Wood)

THE BRITISH

Before going to India, the operational experience of **the Honourable Arthur Wellesley (1769–1852)** had been limited to the Duke of York's fruitless campaign in the Netherlands, as a lieutenant-colonel commanding the 33rd Foot, and then as a brigade commander. Years later he remarked to Lord Stanhope that he had 'learnt what one ought not to do and that is always something.' In 1796 he became colonel of the 33rd Foot and sailed to India with them in the same year. After a successful campaign against Tippu in the Fourth Anglo–Mysore war, where he commanded the Nizam of Hyderabad's force as part of General Harris's army, he was appointed to command in Mysore. He missed the expedition to Egypt due to the 'Malabar itch' and a fever, but commanded the operations against the bandit Doondiah Waugh in 1800 and brought them to a successful conclusion in September of that year. Thereafter his time was spent at Seringapatam administering the newly acquired territory. In 1802 he was appointed to command the British forces gathering at Hurryhur for the restoration of the Maratha Peshwa.

Arthur Wellesley was a very fit, lean, and bright-eyed officer; unusually for the period he drank and ate in moderation and frequently took exercise to keep himself in good shape. He was at home in the saddle and accustomed to riding over all sorts of terrain and thought nothing of riding upwards of 45 miles a day. Like any good commander he was also inquisitive about the country he was operating in and the enemy he would be fighting. Before sailing to India he added 28 books on the country to his library and on the voyage out he studied every day; this approach enabled him to have a store of information about what

Major-General Arthur Wellesley. A miniature painted on his return from India, in the uniform of a colonel of the 33rd Foot. (Victoria & Albert Museum)

General Lord Lake. The commander-in-chief of all British forces in India was a very able general officer and had a string of victories against the Maratha in Hindustan. His most famous victories in 1803 were Delhi and Laswaree. His son, George Lake, standing next to him, was killed at Vimeiro commanding the 29th Foot. (British Library)

had been done in similar situations in the past and this would enable him to react accordingly. On campaign his books and papers were carried in a cart for reference when required. India was the training ground for the future Duke of Wellington; where Napoleon would deride him as a mere 'sepoy general', he himself would happily admit that his military talents were 'all India'.

Colonel James Stevenson (d. 1805) was an East India Company (EIC) cavalry officer who had seen extensive service in India at the time of the 1803 Maratha campaign. He commanded the 1st EIC Cavalry Brigade at Malavelly in 1799 and again led the cavalry in Wellesley's operations in 1800 against the bandit Doondiah Waugh. During his career and like many officers of the time, he would find himself responsible for the administration of large areas of newly acquired territory, and when Wellesley left Seringapatam in late 1800 it was Stevenson who took over the responsibility for the administration of Mysore. He proved to be one of Wellesley's most trusted subordinates, slightly diffident at times, but always reliable. In December 1804 Stevenson sailed for England, but died en route in 1805. He had been promoted to major-general on January 1 that year, but it is unlikely that he had received the news of his promotion.

With the destruction of Tippu at Seringapatam, and with the Mughal emperor Shah Alam a prisoner of Scindia, the **Nizam of Hyderabad** was effectively the last Muslim ruler of an Indian state. Asaf Jah II (1734–1803) had deposed and imprisoned his brother in 1762 and ascended the throne. Asaf Jah II, like many Indian princes, employed European officers to train and command his army. At the start of the campaign against Tippu Sultan in 1799, the Nizam had in his employment 124 Frenchmen, officering 14,000 French troops, who bore the colours of the French Republic and had the Cap of Liberty engraved on their buttons. To confuse the matter further, the subsidiary alliance with Britain also meant there was a force of British troops in the domain at the same time. Not surprisingly the French officers and troops did not sit well with the British, and so before the campaign action was taken to neutralize the French influence; an opportunity arose as a result of mutiny within the French battalions. A show of strength by the British Subsidiary Force and an appeal by Captain Malcolm induced the men to lay down their arms. The officers were sent back to France, while many of the men remained in the Nizam's service and were formed into a new corps led by British officers. In August 1803 Asaf Jah III succeeded his father.

COMMAND AND CONTROL

Napoleon famously called Wellesley 'the sepoy general' which undoubtedly he was early in his career. However, whilst in India Wellesley was able to learn and practise the art of command in battle, which in later years would defeat the very best of Napoleon's Marshals, and the great man himself on the field of Waterloo. His headquarters staff was very small, a theme that was to be continued in the Peninsular War. Captain William Barclay was his adjutant general and as such was responsible for the issue and implementation of regulations and standing orders, discipline, and the collection of reports and returns. In reality, however, Barclay had a far wider remit and at times carried out some of the functions of the quartermaster general, as can be seen in his letter of September 13, 1803 to Colonel Maxwell, where at Wellesley's behest he instructs the said officer to provide an escort and see safely into camp a grain convoy. The majority of the duties of the quartermaster general, such as the conduct of operations, its movement and transport, were carried out by Wellesley himself. As a major-general, Wellesley was entitled to one aide-de-camp (ADC) at the public expense, and in the Deccan campaign this was Captain Colin Campbell of the 78th Highlanders. He had few other staff officers, one exception being Captain John Blakiston, an engineer officer who wrote a wonderful memoir of his time in India and the Peninsula. It was in India that Wellesley learned to take the view that he alone was responsible for the conduct of the army. There is little doubt that his dispatches contain the ideas of his staff officers, but we must remember that once he accepted a piece of advice, the decision to act was his and his alone.

The army in the Deccan was a small and compact one, divided into three small brigades, two infantry and one cavalry, and as a result Wellesley was able to have a far more personal influence on their performance. Wellesley carried out as much personal direction on the battlefield as he could; there were very few commanders who were as cool and able to think as clearly as he was, when the confusion and noise of a battle was at its height. There were three ways in which Wellesley was able to transmit his orders on the battlefield. One of his favoured methods was to arrive in person and give his instructions to the officer concerned. The next most reliable method was to send an officer, one of his ADCs, who would also be able to answer any queries the receiving officer might have. This leads us to the orderly, also used but not as often, as he was quite simply a messenger charged with handing over a note. At the end of the day, however, command is a lonely place and it is the general who decides to give battle or not. The success or failure of his actions would rest squarely on his shoulders.

The Maratha command structure is not as clear. The armies were made up of *compoos* and commanded by a full colonel, whose orders would come directly from his commander. It is unlikely that Scindia's *compoo* commanders would have taken orders from the Raja of Berar and vice versa, as this would have led to unnecessary delays and confusion. Therefore the ability of a local commander, such as a *compoo* commander, to assess a developing situation in front of him and act accordingly, if orders had not been received, was critical; if his actions were successful, all well and good, but if not, the retribution could be severe. On many occasions the Maratha commanders such as Scindia and Berar would absent themselves from the field of battle at a time that suited them, leaving the senior European officer in command.

Wellesley was the commander of a small army, and by being on the spot could assess situations and react accordingly, with great advantages for command and control. The Marathas on the other hand were a coalition army, with the pitfalls of coalition operations to contend with.

Richard Wellesley, 2nd Earl of Mornington (1760–1842). He was an exceptionally able administrator, with great vision and was the architect of the expansion of British influence in India. He was also a vain man who was particularly fond of orders and decorations. (British Library)

Lieutenant-General James Stuart, the commander-in-chief of the Madras forces. He recognized Wellesley's talents and gave him a free hand in the operations that followed. Wellesley recognized what he owed to Stuart and by letter expressed to him his 'strongest sentiments of gratitude, respect, and attachment'. (Print after Lawrence/private collection)

OPPOSING ARMIES

THE MARATHAS

The late 19th- and early 20th-century view of Wellesley's success against the Marathas was one of superior western technology and tactics defeating a large, native Indian army, whose training and manpower was in all respects sub-standard to that of British troops.

The Maratha armies, however, had a sophisticated approach to warfare that was centuries old. They were part of a system of a military economy in India of hiring or being hired as soldiers, which was based on the ever-present threat of armed conflict. Their achievement lay in building up a power base that was to successfully challenge the Mughal empire. The Marathas in the form of warrior bands took service in larger, more cosmopolitan local armies; these armies in turn became more like regional forces in outlook, that were not just concerned with local security but had become large and powerful enough to be regarded as institutions of political control. The Marathas came to dominate this military economy, which enabled them to make a serious bid for political supremacy in South Asia between 1650 and 1817.

The Maratha armies in 1803 were sophisticated organizations. Their employment of mercenaries was based on the requirement for cost-effective combat performance and not on religious or ethnic grounds; the Arabs defending Ahmednugger were Muslim, with a reputation as doughty fighters. They used mercenaries from the lowliest rank to the highest, and it was at the highest level that Europeans were employed. Many, such as De Boigne, George Thomas, Colonel J.P Boyd (an American), and Pohlmann were competent, professional officers who served their masters well. Others were less honourable in their actions and deserted their paymasters, but this was something that the Marathas understood as they too changed sides regularly; being on the winning side was where influence and the greatest profits were to be had. The Europeans over the years had failed to understand the Maratha use of technology and doctrine to give them a competitive edge. The accepted Maratha view was that if a weapon system was more efficient as a killing machine or gave them the ability to shape strategy to win wars, then it was considered with a cold, professional eye. This can be seen in their use of artillery as a means of providing fire superiority on the battlefield. European commentators expressed surprise at the Maratha infantry's ability to manoeuvre at Assaye, yet the use of infantry had a long history in Maratha armies. The use of infantry to secure fortresses helped the great Maratha leader Shivaji Bhonsle to overthrow the

A Maratha horseman. The *tulwar* or sword, carried by Maratha horsemen was razor sharp and capable of decapitating a man, as happened to some of the picquets and 74th Foot at Assaye. (Engraving after James Forbes)

Mughals in western India and gave him a firm base from which to operate. By the middle of the 18th century Maratha doctrine for infantry had evolved, and emphasized the need for infantry to manoeuvre to take advantage of their matchlocks or flintlocks and any superiority that the artillery weapons systems were able to provide. At the Battle of Dabhoi (1731) the Maratha infantry in the army of Peshwa Baji Rao I made use of both column and line, with the latter predominating. At this battle the Marathas integrated their weapons systems to achieve maximum fire effect and used this to give covering fire to their advancing infantry. The battle went unnoticed by the European powers active in India at the time. Lessons were not learnt and misconceptions enhanced.

Maratha infantry

The regular battalions that fought at the Battle of Poona (1802) and in the subsequent campaigns against the British, were the result of the Marathas spending a lot of money and time to ensure their battalions were the best in terms of organization, training, weapons, and discipline. A battalion at this time consisted of two or three European officers, about 40 native officers, and 700 rank and file. Battalion drill movements were based on those of the EIC. They were armed with European flintlock muskets and bayonets, either made in Europe or copied in India. Where there were not enough flintlocks available, battalions were armed with matchlocks. The matchlock was cheaper and easier to produce than the flintlock, but in the hands of a well-trained soldier was equally effective; some commentators at the time said that good matchlock muskets were better than flintlocks. There were four 6-pdr and one 5.5in. howitzer cannon employed as battalion guns, crewed by Indians but commanded by Portuguese gunners, of whom there were six in total. Between four and eight battalions were organized into a brigade, or *compoo*.

Indian infantry that did not have contact with European officers would be armed with almost any weapon they could get their hands on, but particularly spears, bows and arrows, and sub-standard matchlocks.

Maratha cavalry

The Maratha cavalry in the 1803 campaign was probably their weakest arm, yet by far the most numerous. The Marathas employed three classes of cavalry: the first were the *bargirs*, the cream of the cavalry, paid for and maintained by the state. At the death of Shivaji in 1680, they made up two thirds of the cavalry force, yet by the Battle of Panipat in 1761, their numbers had dropped to just 6,000 out of 38,000 cavalrymen. This situation had become no better by the early years of the 19th century as the Marathas continued to put more emphasis on their regular infantry battalions. The second class was that of *silladars*, also employed by the British, who were irregular horse and provided their own horses and weapons – handy for those who wanted to avoid the logistical problems of supplying such items. The final class was the *pindarries*; these were from various ethnic and religious backgrounds, with many being Muslims from the north. Their leader, Amir Khan was a Pathan soldier of fortune. *Pindarries* were an irregular light horse formation who paid a fee or provided their retainers with a percentage, normally one-sixth of any booty taken for the right to plunder. They were used in the military role for screening the movement of troops, reconnaissance, raiding, and

Traditional native soldier. Not all the Maratha infantry were armed with muskets. The more irregular battalions were armed with spears and even bows and arrows. (Engraving by James Forbes)

These are *bargirs*, paid for and maintained by the Maratha state. It was not unusual for the Maratha cavalry to wear chain mail and helmets. (Engraving after Stanley Wood)

cutting supply lines. They were not good against formations of steady infantry or cavalry, but were perfectly capable of cutting up unwary troops. The *pindarries* were armed with a wide assortment and combination of weapons, including swords, lances, muskets and pistols, and bows and arrows.

Maratha artillery

The Maratha artillery was in many respects better than that employed by the British. The weapons were cast all over India in sizes from 1-pdr to 18-pdr cannon and 5in. to 8in. howitzers. There were two reasons why the Marathas employed so many guns against the British. Firstly, it was to make up for the lack of offensive spirit in their infantry when the father-like figures of De Boigne and Perron had departed. The willingness of infantry to advance in battle under enemy fire is directly linked to the example in leadership set by their officers in those circumstances. With the lack of the European officers that normally led the regular infantry battalions, the Marathas used artillery firepower as a substitute for the loss of their infantry's capability. Secondly, they realized that if the air were filled with projectiles, an enemy would be less inclined to advance against their positions with zeal and therefore success. The majority of the guns supporting the regular infantry battalions were 6-pdr and 12-pdr cannon; however, amongst the guns captured at Assaye were weapons of all sizes. The guns were controlled by Portuguese gun captains from Goa, but crewed by Maratha *lascars*.

Although the guns were of a mixture of designs the majority were made of laminated iron and brass; the barrels were far superior to those on British guns. In 1808, tests were carried out at Woolwich on British-made laminated iron barrels, made to the design of a British barrel. The report stated that 'the advantages of the Asiatic ordnance are strength and lightness ... The necessity of resorting to brass guns with iron cylinders ... appears deserving the serious attention of the British Government'. Wellesley wrote after Assaye that 'we have got more than 90 guns, 70 of which are the finest brass ordnance I have ever seen.'

Arab infantrymen. The Arabs were doughty fighters for whoever was their paymaster. They brought their own weapons, in this case muskets, swords, and daggers. (British Library)

Officers of the 19th Light Dragoons, 1798 (left) and 1802–06 (right). The figure on the right is wearing the 'French blue' uniform worn by all King's light cavalry regiments in India at the time. (Watercolour by Charles Stadden/private collection)

THE BRITISH ARMY

The British army in India at this time was made up of King's regiments and those of the East India Company (EIC) presidencies' armies.

The King's regiments

The King's regiments were sent out to India from the home establishment to support the East India Company and its policies. The EIC paid for the King's regiments from the moment they left the shores of Britain until they returned home many years later. Both infantry and cavalry regiments found themselves stationed in India; the artillery did not send out formed units.

The Presidency armies

As the Court of Directors of the EIC realized that they required a military establishment to support their ambitions in India, so the Presidency

armies evolved over a period of time from individual companies to formed battalions, both native and European in composition. The native battalions were recruited from the local populace and no issue was made of caste in the armies of Bombay and Madras; an old *subedar* (officer) of the Madras Army in the 1830s remarked that 'we put our religion into our knapsacks whenever the colours were unfurled'. In the Bengal Army, however, much was made of caste, where only those of the highest caste were admitted. The Presidency armies each had their own nicknames: the Madras Army's was 'the Mulls', from the name of a popular Indian dish, mulligatawny soup. The Bengal (Calcutta) Army were known as the 'Qui-hyes' from the custom of summoning a servant with '*Koi hai?*' meaning 'Is anyone there?' As for the Bombay Army, it had to be the 'Ducks', from the practice of scattering dried fish over curry, known as Bombay duck.

The European battalions were recruited from time-expired soldiers of the King's battalions, who knowing no other life and not wishing to leave India took up service with the EIC. There were two European battalions in each of the presidency armies; eventually they were transferred to the crown and were numbered the 101st to 106th Regiments of Foot.

The infantry

The predominant arm in India was the infantry. The King's and EIC native battalions were organized on similar lines, with only the subtlest of differences. The standard organization of a battalion was of ten companies (eight centre, and two flank companies), with each company having 100 men; in the reality of a campaign, the strength of a company was more likely to be considerably less. The flank companies in a King's battalion were the grenadier company on the right flank and the light company on the left flank. The grenadier companies comprised, ideally, the biggest and strongest men, while the light company was composed of the more nimble and agile soldier who was also a better shot. The EIC battalions differed in that they did not have a light company, but instead had two grenadier companies as their flank companies. The lack of a light company came about as the native Indian soldier was considered a poor skirmisher. Both King's and EIC battalions were commanded by lieutenant-colonels, and companies by a captain. EIC battalions were always commanded by a European, but the companies were commanded by a mix of Indian and European officers. This, however, was changing as the reforms of 1796, which brought to an end the old system of command by native officers, started to take effect.

Both the King's and EIC infantry manoeuvred according to the two books by David Dundas: firstly, the 1788 *Principles of Military Movements Chiefly Applied to Infantry*, and secondly, the *Rules and Regulations for the Movement of His Majesty's Infantry* published in 1792. The King's and EIC (British)

British infantry in India, 1803. From left to right: private, 94th Foot, centre or battalion company; officer, 74th Foot, centre or battalion company; and private, 74th Foot Light Company. (Watercolour By Patrice Courcelle/private collection)

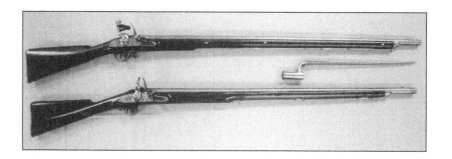

Short Land Pattern musket (top) and India Pattern musket (bottom) with a bayonet (centre). King's regiments arrived in India with the SLP but soon exchanged it for the lighter IP. The latter became the standard issue for British infantry during the Napoleonic Wars. Both were affectionately known as 'Brown Bess'. (SASC/author)

battalions used the system known as the Nineteen Movement; this system allowed a well-drilled battalion to carry out all the evolutions required precisely and without confusion. In battle British infantry fought and manoeuvred in a two-deep line. The advance in line, manoeuvring by the half company, was carried out well by all the British battalions in India; this was as a result of the drill parades executed when in garrison and in camp when on campaign.

By fighting in a two-deep line a British battalion was able to bring all of its firepower to bear on an enemy force. All the companies in King's battalions carried 'Brown Bess' on arrival in India, which weighed approximately 9 lb. with a 42in. barrel. The EIC battalions used the East India Pattern Brown Bess, which was a slightly lighter weapon and had a 39in. barrel. They were both well-made, flintlock, smoothbore muskets, and both weapons in the hands of a well-trained soldier could be fired up to four times a minute. The weapons were not accurate, but at 50 yards a stationary man would be hit almost every time; an enemy unit would receive numerous casualties at 150 yards. Both the King's and EIC battalions handled their muskets well, the result of continual practice, including live firing on ranges. The EIC Pattern Brown Bess soon became the preferred weapon of the King's battalions in India and in due course became the standard musket for British infantry seeing service in Portugal, Spain, and at Waterloo. The bayonet, at 16in. long, was primarily a psychological weapon, but was used with deftness by all British troops when required.

The cavalry

India did not see many King's cavalry regiments, with only the 19th Light Dragoons (LD) serving in the country at the time of the campaign against Tippu Sultan. In this instance, the effectiveness of the 19LD was considerable, and as a result the EIC soon started to raise native cavalry regiments. They were organized, after some initial experimentation, along the lines of a King's regiment, in that they were made up of three squadrons, each of two troops and totalling 517 men in all. A troop at full strength was made up of three British officers, three Indian officers, eight Indian NCOs, a trumpeter, a water carrier, and 70 troopers (privates). The commanding officer was always a European. Like their infantry counterparts the native cavalry were well trained and capable of carrying out the evolutions required to manoeuvre on the battlefield by troop or half troop as well as any European regiment.

The King's and EIC cavalryman was issued with the British light cavalry sabre. This had a curved blade and was much better than comparable enemy weapons. He also carried a carbine and two pistols.

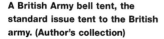

A British Army bell tent, the standard issue tent to the British army. (Author's collection)

Madras infantry and cavalry in camp. (Author's collection)

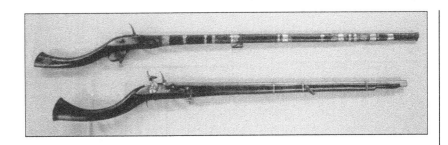

RIGHT **Indian flintlock musket (top) and Indian flintlock rifle (bottom). The rifle has an East India Company lock and the barrel seven deep grooves, but no obvious spiral. (SASC Museum/author's photograph)**

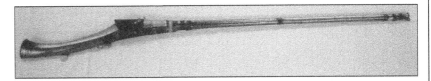

RIGHT **Indian matchlock musket, c.1830. Many Indian soldiers of the native states were armed with matchlocks, which were often better than flintlock muskets – especially with regard to accuracy. (SASC Museum/ author's photograph)**

The King's and EIC regiments were employed as, and had the effect of, heavy cavalry on the battlefield. The charge, delivered at a controlled speed and using their sabres, was executed by squadrons in a two-rank line, with a interval of approximately 15 yards between the two ranks. They were not particularly good at reconnaissance or screening, a complaint levelled at British cavalry throughout the later campaigns against the French in Europe, or in operations against *pindarries*. In the campaign against the Marathas, Wellesley employed his *silladar* horse (irregular cavalry) from Mysore for seeing off the *pindarries* and carrying out the important tasks of reconnaissance and screening. They provided their own horses and were armed with a mixture of weapons including, lances and bows and arrows. They were not suitable for use against formed opposition.

The artillery

There were no King's artillery batteries or companies in India, and so all the artillery support was provided by the EIC. The artillery was organized into companies of five two-gun sections; each section was commanded by a sergeant, with two European gunners and Indian *lascars* (army followers) as gun handlers. In India at this time British infantry battalions still had two guns attached to them; they tended to be 6-pdrs, which gave the battalion more firepower (especially within the range of canister), and a long-range punch against enemy cavalry.

Wellesley in India, as in his later European campaigns, was chronically short of artillery and it was almost certainly here that he learnt how to integrate limited artillery into a tactical plan. He deployed his artillery to operate together in sections of one or more, but Wellesley never attempted to form a grand battery.

BELOW **Madras horse artillery on the move. (Author's collection)**

The artillery pieces used by the British were of the standard Woolwich type, being 3-pdr, 6-pdr, 12-pdr and 5.5in. howitzers. The barrels were cast in England and the wooden field carriages made in India. In 1800 the Madras artillery developed a single trail beam that absorbed the recoil. The 6-pdr and 12-pdr were employed as the standard field artillery piece. The 3-pdr guns were predominantly used for detached service, but were also used as galloper guns attached to the cavalry. In Europe at the time a galloper gun had a split trail, with a single large horse attached directly to it. In India galloper guns were horse drawn, with a gun attached to a limber, and a team of horses attached to the limber. This, in effect, meant that a gun of any size could be used in this role. There were calls by General Stuart for 12-pdr guns to be used in the galloper role; Wellesley, however, did not consider them worth the extra effort and the 6-pdr gun became the accepted option.

Like their infantry and cavalry counterparts, the artillerymen employed in the British armies in India at this time were well-trained professionals and the handling of their guns was of the highest order.

Native infantry and cavalry in 1803. From left to right: private, 4th Madras Native Infantry; *rissaldar* (lieutenant) of the 7th Native Cavalry; and *subedar*, 4th Madras Native Infantry, Grenadier Company. (Watercolour by Patrice Courcelle/private collection)

ORDERS OF BATTLE AT ASSAYE

THE BRITISH ARMY

Army Commander – Major-General the Honourable Arthur Wellesley

Cavalry
**Brigade Commander – Lieutenant-Colonel Patrick Maxwell,
      19th Light Dragoons**
HM 19th Light Dragoons – 384 men (19LD)
4th Native Cavalry – 3 sqns (4NC)
5th Native Cavalry – 3 sqns (5NC)
7th Native Cavalry – 3 sqns (7NC)

Infantry
First Brigade – Lieutenant-Colonel William Wallace, 74th Foot
HM 74th Foot – 1 bn (74)
1/4th Madras Native Infantry – 1 bn (1/4 MNI)
2/12th Madras Native Infantry – 1 bn (2/12 MNI)

Second Brigade – Lieutenant-Colonel William Harness, 80th Foot
HM 78th Foot – 1 bn (78)
1/8th Madras Native Infantry – 1 bn (1/8 MNI)
1/10th Madras Native Infantry – 1 bn (1/10 MNI)

Picquets of the day – Lieutenant-Colonel James Orrock, 1/8 MNI
A half company from each of the battalions – 350 men (PIC)

Naulniah detachment – Lieutenant-Colonel J. Chalmers, 1/2 MNI
1/2nd Madras Native Infantry – 1 bn (1/2 MNI)
Two 6-pdr cannon
Four iron 12-pdr cannon

Artillery
Two 12-pdr cannon attached to the 74th Foot
Ten 6-pdr cannon, two per battalion, attached to each of the remaining infantry
      battalions
Ten 6-pdr galloper cannon; two were attached to the picquets of the day and the
      remainder to the cavalry

Irregular native cavalry
Maharaja of Mysore – 2,400
Maratha – 3,000

Colonel James Stevenson's Subsidiary Force
Cavalry
3rd Native Cavalry – 3 sqns
11th Native Cavalry – 3 sqns

Infantry
HM Scotch Brigade (94th Foot) – 1 bn
2/2nd Madras Native Infantry – 1 bn
1/6th Madras Native Infantry – 1 bn
2/7th Madras Native Infantry – 1 bn
2/9th Madras Native Infantry – 1 bn
11th Madras Native Infantry – 1st and 2nd bn

Artillery
Twelve 6-pdr cannon, two per battalion
Four 6-pdr galloper cannon; two were attached to each of the cavalry regiments

THE MARATHA ARMY

Army Commanders – Maharaja Daulat Rao Scindia; Raja of Berar

Forces of Daulat Rao Scindia

Cavalry
Native *Sirdars* – 12,000 Hindustani and 2,000 Deccani horsemen
Bapoji Scindia (Artillery Park) – 4,000 Hindustani horsemen

Scindia's *Compoos*

Pohlmann *Compoo* **– Colonel Pohlmann**
Regular infantry battalions – 6 (POH)
Cavalry – 500 Hindustani horsemen
Artillery – 40 field guns

Filoze *Compoo* **– Major Dupont**
Regular battalions – 4 (DUP)
Artillery – 20 field guns

Begum Somru *Compoo* **– Colonel Saleur**
Regular battalions – 5 (SAL)
Artillery – 25 field pieces

Artillery
Bapoji Scindia (Artillery Park) – 25 heavy guns, 100 field guns

Forces of Raja of Berar

Cavalry
Native *Sirdars* – 20,000 horsemen

Compoo: **Commander – Beni Singh**
Infantry battalions – 7 (BS)
Artillery – 35 field cannon

Notes:
1. The approximate size of each force engaged at Assaye was:

British Infantry – 5,170 in 7 battalions (incl picquets)
Cavalry – 1,731 in 12 squadrons
Artillery – 22 cannon
Irregular cavalry – 5,400

Maratha – Infantry – 16,000 in 20 battalions
Cavalry – 38,000
Artillery – 245 cannon

2. The British losses, taken from Wellesley's dispatches, were:
European – 164 (killed), 411 (wounded) and 8 (missing);
Native (Madras) – 245 (k), 1,211 (w), 18 (m);
Total: 409 (k), 1,622 (w), 26 (m)

*3. The Maratha losses were not recorded, but British officers such as Blakiston state that there
were 1,200 dead counted on the field of battle. No mention is made of Maratha wounded, however
bearing in mind that the British suffered four times the amount of wounded to killed, and the
weapons systems were on a par, I estimate that the Marathas suffered between 3,600–4,800
wounded.*

4. The Marathas lost 7 brass howitzers, and 69 brass and 22 iron cannon.

THE ROAD TO WAR

THE SCINDIA AND HOLKAR POWER STRUGGLE

The cause for British involvement in Maratha affairs was the defeat of Daulat Rao Scindia and the Peshwa Baji Rao II at the Battle of Poona in October 1802. The battle had been the culmination of a political power struggle between the two most powerful Maratha chiefs, Jaswant Rao Holkar of Indore and Daulat Rao Scindia, for influence over the Peshwa. The Peshwa was the chief minister of the Marathas and held political power in the Maratha confederation. The victor, Holkar, had marched into Poona in triumph after the battle, but the political prize, in the form of the Peshwa, eluded him. In being defeated, Scindia had not only lost the battle, but also his control over Baji Rao who had fled before the end of the fighting. Baji Rao's flight took him into British territory and his request for British protection opened the door for British involvement in Maratha internal politics. The Governor General Lord Mornington agreed, fearing French involvement if the British refused to help. The result was the Treaty of Bassein, signed on December 31, 1802.

Through the treaty the British entered into a subsidiary alliance with the nominal head of the Maratha confederacy. Three of the most important provisions were: (1) the subsidiary force was to consist of five battalions and artillery, and was to be stationed within the Peshwa's territory in perpetuity; (2) the Company was to control the Peshwa's dealings with other states and, more importantly, was to act as arbitrator in any disputes, present or future, with Hyderabad; (3) the Peshwa was to take no Europeans into service without the leave of the British. The treaty was far more than just another subsidiary alliance as henceforward the East India Company was committed to either controlling the greatest Indian power, or coming to blows with it.

POLITICAL AND MILITARY MANOEUVRING

The months following the signing of the Treaty of Bassein were filled with protracted diplomatic activity, coupled with military preparation. After the Battle of Poona, Holkar, who had wanted not to depose Baji Rao as Peshwa but instead become the power behind him, now tried to put his own man Vinayak Rao, the son of Amrat Rao, upon the throne; at the same time, he wished to demonstrate cordial feelings towards the British Government and endeavoured to obtain from them a recognition of his proposal. The British as part of the Treaty of Bassein had agreed to restore Baji Rao to his

The fort of Bassein. Baji Rao came to Bassein after asking the British for assistance, and subsequently signed the treaty of that name. (British Library)

capital city; this, however, required the removal of Holkar from Poona while at the same time Lord Mornington also hoped to offer the other Maratha leaders, but not necessarily including Holkar, a position within the subsidiary alliance system. The conduit for British policy towards the Marathas was Barry Close, who had remained as British Resident in Poona at Holkar's request. Close made what turned out to be three correct assumptions: firstly, that the Maratha feudatories of the Peshwa in the south would continue to give some measure of support to him; secondly, because of the depth of their personal dispute and the geographical distance between their forces, that Holkar and Scindia would not combine against the British; and thirdly, that Holkar would withdraw from Poona without a fight.

Although Wellesley had been sent orders in November 1802 to start assembling and concentrating a force of 'observation' on the Tombuddra, the British hoped to restore the Peshwa to Poona without a fight. There was some prospect that this avenue might be possible (as Holkar had remained friendly to the British) and that Scindia might favour the British restoring the Peshwa, particularly as in early 1802 the Gaikwar of Baroda, another Maratha chief, had been successfully restored to his capital by a small force of the Bombay Army. The force being assembled by Wellesley would be made up of troops from Madras and from Seringapatam and concentrate on the Mysore–Maratha border, while the remainder would come from Hyderabad.

Meanwhile, negotiations with the Marathas continued and Barry Close was discovering the difficulty of working with Baji Rao. He was reminded each day of the hatred that Baji Rao had for his half-brother, Amrat Rao, and for Holkar. This hindered any attempt by the British to negotiate in the disputes between the Marathas. As time went by Close began to realize that Baji Rao's attitude to his new alliance with the British was guarded and even disingenuous. Baji Rao was anxious at all times to do nothing that might discourage Scindia from returning to Poona, for if this was to happen his restoration would be affected without help from the British and therefore he would be freed of any obligation to them. Close realized that, faced with a decision, Baji Rao would take refuge in delay, hoping that changes in the rapidly shifting political scene would

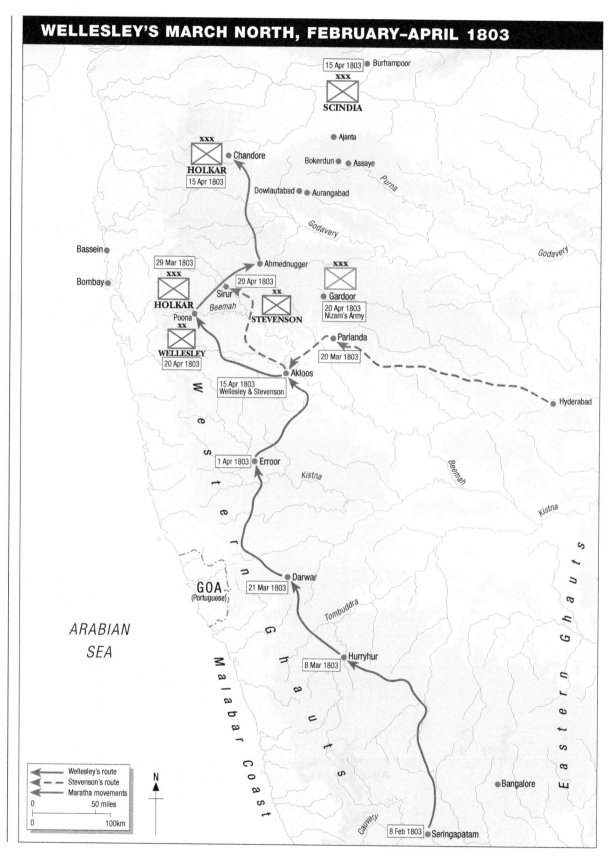

15 Apr 1803 • Burhampoor

xxx
SCINDIA

• Ajanta

xxx
Bokerdun • • Assaye
HOLKAR • Chandore
15 Apr 1803

Dowlautabad • • Aurangabad
Purna

Godavery

Godavery

Bassein •

29 Mar 1803
xxx
HOLKAR   Ahmednugger •   xxx
Bombay •   20 Apr 1803
Sirur •   xx   Gardoor •
Beemah   STEVENSON   20 Apr 1803
Poona •   Nizam's Army
xx
WELLESLEY   Parianda •
20 Apr 1803   20 Mar 1803
Akloos •
15 Apr 1803
Wellesley & Stevenson   Hyderabad •

W
e
s
t
e
r
n

1 Apr 1803 • Erroor
Kistna   *Beemah*

Kistna

G
h
a
u
t
s

E
a
s
t
e
r
n

GOA
(Portuguese)
Darwar •
21 Mar 1803   *Tombuddra*

ARABIAN
SEA   Hurryhur •
8 Mar 1803

*M
a
l
a
b
a
r*

*C
o
a
s
t*   Bangalore •   G
h
a
u
t
s

Wellesley's route
Stevenson's route
Maratha movements
0   50 miles
0   100km   N   *Cauvery*   8 Feb 1803 • Seringapatam

A British army on the march. Although not in the Deccan, it is very similar to that place. Note the officers in the foreground wearing hats and the general's entourage just above them. (British Library)

Poona, the capital of the Peshwa and of the Maratha Confederation. (Print after George Rowley/private collection)

bring a variation on a theme and make any course of action clearer. Had Baji Rao been more active, there is every possibility that he would have succeeded in manoeuvring the EIC to his own advantage; however, the advantage went to the British, for he was too indolent for such a venture. It soon became evident that the British could deal with Baji Rao as one chief among many Maratha chiefs, or as the first civil officer of the Maratha empire. It was also not for the British to determine in what capacity Baji Rao had signed the Treaty of Bassein, for there was no guarantee that the major Maratha chiefs would view the alliance as being signed by the Peshwa on behalf of the Maratha confederation. The actions of the three major chiefs – Holkar, Scindia, and Raghuji Bhonsle (Raja of Berar) – would in the end determine its significance and validity. It was the realization of this that in February 1803 prompted Mornington to report to the Secret Committee of the Court of Directors that 'the complete operation' of the Treaty of Bassein was 'still subject to doubt' and that the Maratha chiefs were 'averse to an alliance between the British Government and the sovereign power of the Maratha empire.'

In January 1803 Barry Close had reported that Holkar had quarrelled with Amrat Rao over Amrat Rao's inability to seize the resources of Poona and the surrounding area in order to placate the demand for plunder of Holkar's forces. In February Amrat Rao wrote to the Governor of

Bombay and although nothing came of the approach, it was deemed a further indication that Holkar's demands on the Peshwa were such that he was unable to deal with them. This was confirmed when Close reported that Holkar faced serious difficulties over resources, stating:

> From the territory north of Poona he can derive nothing, as he has made it a desert, and to attempt to penetrate to the southward for subsistence for his numerous cavalry and banditti … would result in serious opposition.

Despite a near mutinous situation brought on by a lack of resources, Holkar still had a formidable force at Poona; Barry Close reported it as 56,000 cavalry, 15,900 infantry, and 157 guns of various calibres. Close tried to discuss Holkar's demands with Baji Rao's principal minister Raghunath Rao, but had it explained to him that the Peshwa viewed Holkar as a traitor and that no instructions would be sent to Scindia, who alone could meet any demand, to satisfy them. In early March Barry Close received instructions from Mornington in Fort William, Calcutta, suggesting that an attempt should be made to reconcile Baji Rao with Holkar. On receiving these instructions, Close delayed implementing them, pending confirmation of the movements of Wellesley's detachment that was to march into Maratha territory from Mysore. When Close finally approached Baji Rao he was met once again with an absolute refusal by Baji Rao to permit any approach to Holkar. Close had to inform Holkar that the British intended to invoke the Treaty of Bassein and restore Baji Rao to Poona as the Peshwa.

We must now look at the role played by Scindia. In November 1802 Scindia, in a letter to Mornington, indicated that he was going to move into the Deccan with the object of 'arranging the disordered affairs of that quarter', and also expressed the hope that he would be included in any negotiations with the Peshwa. Mornington directed Colonel John Collins to return as British Resident with Scindia's court, or *darbar*. At the same time he replied to Scindia that the restoration of Collins as the Resident was to co-ordinate means of restoring peace. During the month of March Collins had two audiences with Scindia. In the first, on March 11, he reported the fact of the Treaty of Bassein and that the British intended to restore Baji Rao to Poona, putting forward two proposals from Mornington: (1) British

Madras sepoys on the march with their *puckalees* (the water-carriers attached to King's and native regiments). Kipling's Gunga Din was a water-carrier. (Pen and ink by David Rowlands/private collection)

Bullock train. The majority of the baggage train was pulled by bullocks. Captain MacKay the bullock master for Wellesley, against orders, fought at Assaye and was killed. (Engraving after Stanley Wood)

mediation in the dispute between Scindia and Holkar; and (2) the making of an alliance similar to that recently undertaken with Baji Rao. The second audience happened on March 24 at which Collins detected that the *darbar* was not at all in favour of Mornington's proposals. Collins realized that Scindia was dissatisfied with the part played by the British in the affairs of the Maratha empire and challenged him to disclose his real intentions. Scindia's ministers argued that Baji Rao should have consulted Scindia before agreeing to a treaty with the British. Scindia then asked Collins for the terms of the Treaty of Bassein. Collins, who was sure that Scindia must have had an idea of the detail, agreed, provided that Scindia would allow him to discuss the different articles with the intention of Scindia becoming part of the general defensive alliance. The approach favoured by Collins was blocked by Scindia's ministers; when writing to Mornington, Collins correctly surmised that they would continue to block any British approaches, and that in the end the Peshwa would only be restored by the actions of the British administration. The unhelpful attitude of Scindia and his ministers played into the hands of Close, whose preoccupation was that of a military advance and not negotiation with the Maratha confederacy; with the British and the British alone placing Baji Rao back as Peshwa in Poona.

Arthur Wellesley received word from General Stuart of his appointment to command the force to restore the Peshwa in the first week of March. His orders were to encourage the southern *jagirdars* (landowners) to declare in favour of the Peshwa's cause; to concentrate at Miraj with the Hyderabad subsidiary force under the command of Colonel Stevenson; effect a junction with the Peshwa; and march on Poona to 'establish an order of things in that capital favourable to the return of the Peshwa'. As the British troops crossed the Tombuddra River into Maratha territory on March 11, Wellesley wrote to his brother: 'all your plans will be carried into execution'. Strict instructions had been issued that Maratha territory was to be considered friendly and that looters would meet summary justice of flogging or hanging. The first problem to confront the British force was Darwar; Wellesley could not afford to lay siege to the place with the predicted casualties, and so the decision was taken to bypass. With the British column moving north quickly, but well within its logistical constraints and in good health, they soon saw the wastage of the countryside caused by Holkar's forces. At the end of March, Close reported to Wellesley that once again Baji Rao was being obdurate, this time refusing to join the Company detachment. A few days later in early April Wellesley became aware that Holkar was withdrawing from Poona, northwards towards Ahmednugger. On April 15 the forces of Wellesley and Stevenson were both close to Akloos, but did not unite. Wellesley rode over to Stevenson's camp to discuss the campaign; it was decided that initially the two forces would act separately as a new report indicated that Holkar had gone to his only hereditary stronghold in the Deccan, Chandore. Wellesley's intelligence system was soon reporting that Holkar had definitely reached Chandore and that only Amrat Rao remained in Poona,

British troops on the march, drawn by Lieutenant Layard in 1843 in the Scinde. In 1798 Colonel Bayly wrote: 'I had two bullocks laden with biscuits, two with wine and brandy, two with my trunks, and four for the marquee'. (British Library)

but the rumours were that he was going to plunder and torch the city as the British approached. On April 19 the British army completed its customary 20-mile march and by 1pm had bivouacked. To ensure that Amrat Rao's threat to plunder the city did not happen, Wellesley decided to make a bold dash for Poona with the cavalry, a sepoy battalion, the 2/12 MNI, and a full complement of cavalry gallopers. Not all went perfectly well, for the gallopers became stuck in the Little Bore Ghaut. The sepoy battalion remained at the foot of the Ghaut, as the cavalry, having dashed 60 miles in 32 hours, arrived in Poona in the early afternoon of April 20. The surprise was complete and the city was taken without a fight, with Amrat Rao leaving through one gate as Wellesley arrived through another. Within a few days the rest of Wellesley's force arrived at Poona. In early May a strong force from Bombay brought Baji Rao to the vicinity of his capital, but being superstitious he would not enter the city until the stars were aligned properly, which they were on May 13.

With the restoration of the Peshwa, Scindia realized that his own influence in Poona had gone and he started to negotiate secretly with the other Maratha chiefs, particularly Holkar and Berar. Holkar, however, did not intrigue with Scindia and the alliance was formed with Berar. In the north some of Scindia's forces were reported as crossing the Nerbudda River and, although still very distant, Wellesley's intelligence sources assessed the movement to be one that also threatened Poona. Although the hope was for a negotiated settlement, the military preparations continued. Mornington instructed Collins to ask Scindia what his intentions were, and when asked what his position was regarding the Treaty of Bassein, Scindia replied that he would have to ask Berar. This reply was not deemed suitable and it became clear in a letter from Collins that it was unlikely that Scindia could be persuaded that the subsidiary alliance system was advantageous to him. In late May and early June 1803 it seemed that armed confrontation was inevitable between the British and the Marathas under Scindia and Berar, but the tense stand-off was to continue for another two months.

THE CAMPAIGN OF ASSAYE

ARMED CONFRONTATION

Wellesley marched out of Poona on June 4 towards the Godavery River; his aim was to be in a position to react to any hostile movements by Scindia and Berar, who had assembled their forces at Burhampoor on the Taptee, with the intention of invading the Nizam of Hyderabad's domains. Berar's force consisted of 20,000 cavalry, ten battalions of infantry (6,000 men), and 40 pieces of artillery. On the same day Collins was at a *durbar* (meeting) with Scindia and his ministers at Burhampoor. At the meeting Collins urged Scindia to remove any doubt as to his intentions; Scindia would not do so, saying that only after he had discussed matters with the Raja of Berar would he be able to tell Collins whether it was to be peace or war. When Wellesley heard of this he was concerned that Scindia had delayed giving Collins a definite answer and suggested that the answer that he had given 'might justify an immediate attack upon the possession of Scindia'. Wellesley, when writing to Mornington, the Governor General, wrote, 'I have urged the Colonel [Collins] to press Scindia to name a day on which he will explain his intentions, and if Scindia should decline to name a day he should fix one for him, beyond which in my opinion he ought not to remain in his [Scindia's] camp'. At the same time Wellesley in a letter to Calcutta deplored the fact that he was not delegated powers to 'act at once'. This was a reference to the fact that it took six weeks for dispatches to do a round trip between the Deccan, via Hyderabad to Calcutta.

Over the next few days Wellesley's main problem was military. He had not received any reinforcement of his forces by the southern *jagirdars*. He needed these horsemen to shield his slower moving force from the

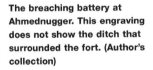

The breaching battery at Ahmednugger. This engraving does not show the ditch that surrounded the fort. (Author's collection)

silladar and *pindarry* horsemen of Scindia and Berar. The reason for not receiving these reinforcements could simply be put down to the deliberate procrastination of Baji Rao. Wellesley was becoming impatient with Baji Rao's 'incapacity for business' and wrote to Close that 'the alliance in its present form, and with the present Peshwa, will never answer'. He now suggested that thought should be given to withdrawing from the alliance, 'with honour and safety'.

Heavy monsoon rains were now disrupting the negotiations; Collins had three feet of water in his dining tent and the stream between Scindia and Berar was impassable. When the weather relented Collins sent Scindia a letter reminding him of his promised reply and that any further delay would be taken as evidence of his intention 'to obstruct the completion of the Treaty of Bassein, either by means of his own power, or in conjunction with Raghuji Bhonsle [Raja of Berar] and Holkar'. The response from Scindia was that no reply could be given until a meeting had taken place with not only Holkar but also the Peshwa. Collins did not leave the camp but remained to try to reach a peaceful settlement with Scindia.

In his camp near Ahmednugger, which was garrisoned by Scindia's troops, Wellesley was confident that a decision whether it was to be war or peace could not be far away. On June 14 he moved Stevenson's force forward, but not 'to go a great distance from Aurangabad ... before I can cross the Godavery and give you support.' Wellesley remained south of the Godavery with the intention of capturing Ahmednugger, which would provide a secure base from which to operate, and was also 'full of everything we want'. On July 17 Wellesley received his brother's order dated June 26 giving him full military and political authority. He instructed Collins, who was still in Scindia's camp north of Ajanta, to have another *durbar* with Scindia and Berar and to speak plainly. He was to explain the detail of the Treaty of Bassein and to ask exactly what their objection to it was. Collins was also to explain that he was prepared to make concessions but that the Maratha forces must be withdrawn from the borders of the Nizam's territories. In essence, their time was up. At the *durbar* on July 29 Collins was firm in his dealings with Scindia and Berar, and as they could give no reason for their forces being on the Nizam's borders, told them to withdraw. There was some discussion during which the Marathas tried to negotiate a mutual withdrawal of the British back to their cantonments, but Collins saw it for what it was – procrastination – and reported to Wellesley that he had been unable to secure the satisfaction that had been demanded of Scindia and Berar as to what their intentions were. Collins left Scindia's camp with a large escort and headed south to the Nizam's city of Aurangabad. Word reached Wellesley on August 6 of the failed diplomatic negotiations while he was at Waklee, having encamped there to wait for a break in the monsoon. On August 7 Wellesley informed Scindia and Berar that, as they had refused the terms offered to them and chosen war, the responsibility lay with them for the consequences of any conflict.

THE ESCALADE OF AHMEDNUGGER

Wellesley had determined early on that the first act of any war was to be the capture of Ahmednugger. Consequently on the morning of August 7 his order was issued for the army to march the seven miles there, but it was rescinded as the heavy monsoon rains had not abated. On August 8, however, the day was bright and clear and the British army made the short march in two hours. During the time he had been encamped close to Ahmednugger, Wellesley, when taking his daily rides for exercise, had examined the town and fort on numerous occasions and so had a good idea in his mind of its strength and how he would deal with it when the time came. The potential for the town to provide a base to guard Poona and for the projection of power into the Deccan had not been lost on Wellesley. There were other reasons why the town was important: firstly, it was a well-fortified stronghold and was therefore ideal as a logistical hub for any operations; secondly, it would be an ideal location for troops to rest and recover from the ravages of campaigning, if the situation became all out war with the Marathas; thirdly, it was a good base for any counter-insurgency operations that might have to be undertaken against *pindarries*; and fourthly, it would be useful if there were a requirement in the future to pacify the Peshwa or Nizam. The town was surrounded by the *pettah* (town) wall, which was some 18ft high, rounded at the top, and with small circular bastions, every 100 yards, mounted with wall pieces (guns) at regular intervals. The fort, which was one of the strongest in India, was outside the *pettah*. The fort was almost circular in shape and made of stone, with a wide and deep ditch all the way around it. The bastions were large and at short intervals and sitting atop them were upwards of 60 cannon ranging from 12- to 52-pdrs.

On the 8th Wellesley rode ahead of his army with Bisnapah, the commander of his Mysore irregular cavalry, and a squadron of the 19th Light Dragoons. A letter was sent to the *killadar* or commandant of the fort requesting its surrender, which was met with a not unexpected refusal. A request to offer the *pettah* protection if it were to accept occupation was also refused. The *pettah* was garrisoned by 1,200–1,500 Arabs, who were not amenable to discipline and fought as individuals; they were employed by the Marathas for guarding forts, which they always defended with great valour. According to Captain Welsh, who was at

The memorial to the 78th Highlanders at Ahmednugger. (Author's collection)

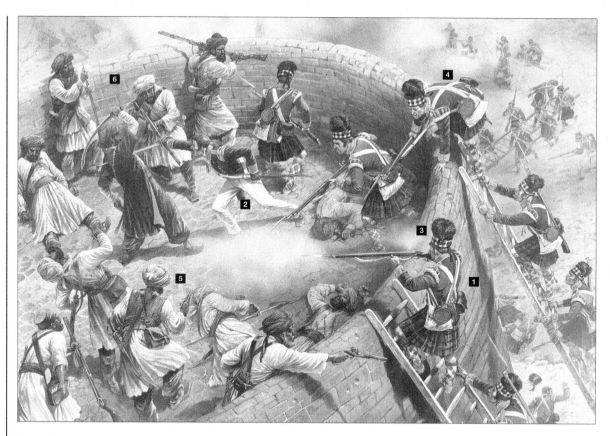

THE ESCALADE OF AHMEDNUGGER *PETTAH* WALLS
(pages 38–39)

Lieutenant Colin Campbell and the Grenadier Company of the 78th Highlanders gain a foothold on one of the bastions of Ahmednugger's *pettah* wall. Wellesley decided that the best way was to carry out an escalade (1). An escalade is when troops assault a fortified place using ladders to mount the walls. The act of carrying out an escalade was considered a very risky kind of 'surprise' attack. Successful escalades were dependent on several factors: the attackers had to achieve surprise, by the timing and location of the attack; the troops had to attack in several columns, so that the chances of success were increased, by hopefully attacking a weakly defended part of the wall; and lastly, once over the walls the attackers had to get around to the town gates and open them, so that the main force was able to enter the town. The initial British attacks against the *pettah* wall were not successful and it could be argued that the element of surprise had been lost. The first man to obtain a foothold on the tower, once the point of attack had been changed to the bastions, was Lieutenant Colin Campbell (2). Campbell was the lieutenant in the Grenadier Company and assumed command when his company commander, Captain Huddlestone, had been killed in the first assault. He was commissioned as an ensign into the 1st West India Regiment in October 1799 and then had the usual CV of his time for officers: lieutenant (35th Foot)

August 1801, exchanging (transferring) into the 78th Highlanders in February 1802. He was noted for his gallantry at Ahmednugger, was appointed ADC to Wellesley the very next day, and was promoted to captain. He also fought at the battles of Assaye and Argaum. He served on the staff of Wellesley in the Peninsular War and at Waterloo, rising in rank from captain to colonel in that time. In 1838 he became a lieutenant-general and governor of Ceylon. He died in 1847. There is much conjecture as to whether Highland regiments retained the kilt in India (3). It is possible that the 78th was still kilted, while other Highland regiments very quickly adopted linen trousers. British troops in India did not march with their knapsacks (4), they were carried in the battalion baggage, whereas the EIC native battalions did march with their knapsacks. The Marathas employed Arab mercenaries (5) to garrison their fortresses. This employment of Arabs, who were Muslims, is typical of the Marathas' paying for the right type of soldier to do a certain job, regardless of religion. They were doughty fighters and ideally suited to fortress warfare. They wore traditional Arab dress in white/off-white, with leather belts and cross straps. Each man was armed with an assortment of weapons (6). The favoured firearm was the matchlock, more accurate than a flintlock and easier to get hold of. The pistol and sword were also a common element of an Arab soldier's arsenal. Spears were carried if no matchlocks or flintlocks were available. (Peter Dennis)

A bazaar in Scindia's camp. This is the sort of scene that would have greeted 'Little King Collins' on each of his visits for a *darbar* with Scindia. (Author's collection)

Ahmednugger and wrote of his experience in his *Military Reminiscences*, there were some 3,000 Maratha light horsemen between the fort and the *pettah*, presumably to provide support to the Arabs in the *pettah*. The horsemen soon dispersed, however.

Wellesley's plan was divided into two phases: the first was to attack and capture the *pettah*, as this would then provide an ideal platform for the second phase, which would be the siege of the fortress itself. Wellesley placed himself on a small, elevated spot, within long gunshot range of both places and determined that the place could be carried by escalade. The length of the relatively low wall, some 4,000 yards long with 40 bastions, meant that the 1,500-odd Arabs could not guard it at all places. He surmised that the town might have a militia of sorts, but this would not be particularly well armed or led and therefore of little consequence. He issued orders for the escalade to be carried out by three mutually supporting assault columns. The first was to be the picquets of the day, who were to assault the wall to the left of the gateway. This composite battalion was made up of a half company from each of the King's regiments and from each of the sepoy battalions of the Madras Native Infantry (MNI); a total of one company of Europeans and two and a half companies of sepoys, commanded by the field officer of the day. They were to receive assistance from the flank companies of the 78th Foot and would be commanded by Colonel Harness of the 80th Foot. The second column was to comprise the battalion companies of the 74th Foot, supported by the 1/8 MNI and commanded by Lieutenant-Colonel Wallace of the 74th Foot. This column would be the central attacking column, and would attack the gateway itself by taking a gun forward with them; they would put the muzzle of the gun against the outer surface of the heavy wooden gate and blow it off its hinges. The task of the third column, made up of the 1/3 MNI and the flank companies of the 74th Foot, was to assault the wall to the right of the gateway. It was commanded by Captain Vesey of the MNI battalion. The two columns tasked to attack the walls were issued with scaling ladders. Lieutenant-Colonel Adams, commanding the 78th Foot, in a letter to Major-General Mackenzie Fraser dated August 17, 1803 also states that the central column was principally intended as a feint and that 'the guns of the cavalry were ordered to cannonade the wall, and one or

Even in the dry season the wheat fields on the banks of the Godavery River are in a healthy state. Wellesley did not live off the land, and would have paid for any produce. (Author's photograph)

The Godavery River near Toka. It took three days for the British army to cross the Godavery in wicker boats. (Author's photograph)

two regiments of native infantry made some feints to distract the enemy's attention'. The Arabs, dressed in white with white turbans and with their weapons and accoutrements glinting in the sun, waited for the assault to begin.

What Wellesley did not know was that the *pettah* wall had been constructed without a rampart behind its exterior curtain wall. In other words there was no walkway inside the top of the *pettah* wall where the assaulting troops would expect to find one. The picquets of the day, along with the flank companies of the 78th Foot, were at the front of the column of march, and halted about a mile from the *pettah* at about 9am. Captain James Fraser of the 78th Foot, commanding his regiment's flank companies, put the time of the first assault, which was to get off to a rather poor start, at about 10am. After advancing the final mile the picquets halted some 60 yards from the wall and flanking bastions, opposite the place that was to be the point of the assault and deployed into line. They were to give supporting fire to the flank companies of the 78th Foot, who

carried forward their ladders and placed them against an undefended part of the wall between the two bastions. The Grenadier Company, led by Captain Huddlestone, went up one ladder and the Light Company, commanded by Captain Grant, up another in, as Lieutenant-Colonel Alexander Adams wrote, 'a most gallant manner'. The cross fire from the Arabs in the two bastions was heavy and very accurate and as the two officers reached the top of their ladders they were hit by the musket fire; both fell dead. The picquets did their best to keep the heads of the defenders down, but as the troops reached the top of the ladders and found nowhere to alight they bunched up and made an easy target for the defenders. The attackers struggled on for ten minutes, but as the casualties mounted they were forced to withdraw. The stout Highlanders were not to be defeated so easily, and were soon back into the attack. This time the two flank companies set their ladders at the foot of the bastions next to the wall they had failed to carry. The first man up one of the ladders was Lieutenant Colin Campbell, now commanding the Grenadier Company, who with sword in hand was wounded and fell off the ladder. The soldiers following him were cleared off the ladder by a shower of rocks and other projectiles. Campbell once again started up the ladder, only to meet the same fate as before. On the third occasion he allowed his claymore to hang from his wrist and encouraging his men to follow him as quickly as they could, dashed up the ladder and successfully reaching the top he leapt over the heads of the Arab defenders at the parapet. Wellesley watched as the brave Campbell began to lay about the defenders with his claymore, and was quickly followed by his grenadiers. There was a short, sharp fight and the bastion was cleared. The Highlanders made their way down to the ground floor and having emerged from the inner doorway, were charged by some Arabs; once again a short sharp fight ensued with Campbell wielding his claymore to great effect, some of his men discharging their still-loaded muskets and all his men using their bayonets in a deadly fashion.

The assaults further along the wall had similar problems. As the right-hand assault party advanced towards the *pettah* wall it came under artillery fire support from the fort. A gun-elephant, taking fright at the shot from the fort, ran amok down the centre of the column, which caused much confusion and allowed the enemy more time to prepare for

Rackisbaum, one of the entrances to the village still standing. (Author's photograph)

the attack. Having recovered their composure the assault went in, with ladders being placed against the curtain wall at the re-entering angle formed by a small bastion. The first attempt was made under heavy and accurate fire from the Arab defenders and was such a rush that one of the ladders broke due to overloading, forcing the troops to use the second ladder only. Captain Vesey of the 1/3 MNI was leading the assault, with Captain Welsh as one of his officers, who in a typically soldierly way saw the humour in the situation and wrote: 'Captain Vesey was then a very stout and heavy man; but what impediment, short of death, can arrest a soldier at such a crisis?' Captain Vesey was soon up on the bastion closely followed by his men, all determined to carry everything before them. The two flank companies of the 74th Foot had both scrambled up the ladder, as had 150–200 sepoys of the 1/3 MNI, when a cannon ball smashed the last ladder, leaving those on the bastion to their own devices. Captain Welsh describes what they did next: 'dashing down we scoured all the streets near the wall, the enemy only once making a stand, and suffering accordingly.' Resistance was beginning to collapse as the momentum swung in favour of the British troops who were now making their way towards the main gate. The enemy at the gate were soon driven off and as some of the sepoys of the 1/3 MNI started to open the gate, the cannon belonging to Colonel Wallace's party went off in their faces, leaving many with burning clothing and singed hair, but only one sepoy dead. The parties united under the command of Colonel Wallace and started about clearing the town of the defenders and with this successfully done at about 3pm the town was in British hands. The Arab troops were prevented from reaching the fort by British and allied cavalry who forced them to withdraw to the north, harassing them on their way. There was a little plundering and rape, but Wellesley promptly had a sepoy hanged on the side of the captured gate as an example to his European and Indian troops. It has been suggested that Wellesley did this in order to keep the Maratha people friendly to the British, or neutral at best, and whilst there is some truth in this, he also did it because he was a disciplinarian and simply would not tolerate his soldiers behaving in such a vile manner.

The record of losses by the British is confusing, with Thorn, who was not there, giving 30 killed and 111 wounded; Grant Duff giving 28 killed but only 22 wounded; and Captain Welsh, who was there, giving a total loss of 160 men. The return for the 78th Foot, given in a letter home written by the commanding officer indicates 14 killed and 41 wounded, which suggests that the estimates of Thorn and Welsh are more accurate.

As befitting a general of his time, Wellesley had a sizeable dining tent, which was put up during the assault and where afterwards he entertained many officers to, what was for most of them no doubt, their first meal of the day. Wellesley had with him at this time two Maratha chieftains, Goklah and Appah Dessaye, who were commanding some 4,000 cavalry on behalf of the Peshwa. Goklah wrote to a friend:

> *These English are a strange people, and their General a wonderful man. They came here in the morning, looked at the pettah wall, walked over it, killed all the garrison, and returned to breakfast! What can withstand them?*

THE CAPITULATION OF THE FORTRESS

Although the *pettah* had fallen and provided the base that Wellesley needed, the fortress was still in Maratha hands. He carried out a reconnaissance of the fortress on the evening of August 9, whilst some of his troops seized a minor outer work some 400 yards from its walls. It soon became apparent to Wellesley that the fort was very strong and would not fall to an escalade; siege was the only option. Having carefully selected the section of wall to be breached, he gave orders for a breaching battery of four 12-pdr cannon to be set up during the night some 300 yards from the fort. At dusk he paraded all the pioneers with their implements and set them to work constructing the battery position under the guidance of Captain Johnson of the Engineers and Captain Heitland of the Pioneers. All was not plain sailing, as the Maratha artillerymen on the walls of the fort started firing illumination rounds, some of which comprised the burning carcasses of animals, with the aim of providing light so that Arab marksmen could snipe at the construction party. Extra picquets were posted as a precaution to stop a sally from the fort, but also to deal with any Arab foot patrols trying to probe the lines. By next morning the pioneers had completed their task and provided an excellent battery position with good cover for the guns and crews.

In the early morning of August 10 the battery of four 12-pdrs opened fire. Wellesley first wanted to neutralize the Maratha cannon on the wall that had been selected for breaching. The reason for this was that, although the guns ranged in size, the most noteworthy was the Maha Laxim, a bronze cannon measuring 22ft in length and firing a 17-pdr ball. The breaching battery was in range of all these guns, therefore they had to be dealt with before the business of weakening the wall and forming a breach could begin.

By late afternoon on August 11 a breach had begun to appear, but was far from being completed, and the guns were running out of ammunition. Wellesley could not order a storming of the fort as it still had not been worked out how to attack the fort with scaling ladders that were too short to be used inside the ditch, and more importantly how to plant them in 10ft of water.

Wellesley decided to use bluff and money. The *killadar* had been negotiating for a capitulation since the afternoon of August 10; on August 12, to help him make up his mind, Wellesley paraded a storming party at the same time as offering a negotiated financial settlement. On the same day the fortress capitulated to the British and the garrison marched out; Ahmednugger fortress had remained impregnable for 300 years, only to fall to four 12-pdr cannon and bluff. Welsh's recollections proves that soldiers have short memories:

A wild scene of disorder followed, soldiers and sepoys all taking part in plundering Scindia's palace ... nor did the looting cease until two native soldiers had been seized and summarily hanged in the gateway of the palace.

The fortress was quickly repaired and Wellesley brought forward from Poona the 2/3 MNI under Major Kennet and a platoon from the 84th Foot to act as gun handlers for a brigade of guns, to garrison Ahmednugger. With his base for operations secure Wellesley was ready to carry out the second part of his plan – to cross the Godavery River and bring the Marathas to battle.

CHASING DOWN SCINDIA AND BERAR

The first units to leave Ahmednugger did so on August 14 when Wellesley sent ahead an advance party and all the cavalry to the stretch of river they were to cross at Toka. Their task was to secure the crossing site and to make enough wicker boats from *sambalu*, a kind of willow, and leather for the army to cross in. The boats were ready on August 20 and Wellesley arrived with the main army on August 22; on August 25 the army had crossed the Godavery and was continuing its march to Aurangabad. Stevenson with his force had been north of the Godavery since May and at this time was at Jafarabad with the task of intercepting the Maratha *pindarries* that had entered the Nizam's territories. The *pindarries* were soon causing discomfort to Stevenson, who found himself scrabbling to discover their whereabouts and fending off their hit-and-run raids against the supply convoys. Wellesley arrived at Aurangabad on August 29 and took stock of the situation. On his arrival he took a party of officers to see Colonel Collins, the late British resident at Scindia's court, who was encamped just north of Aurangabad. Captain Blakiston, who was Wellesley's engineer, joined the cortège going to see Collins and remarked as he rode through the town that there was no building of any consequence except a mausoleum, 'a beautiful structure entirely of white marble, justly admired for the elegance of its design'. On arriving at the camp of Collins they were met with a three-gun salute of artillery. Blakiston describes the scene:

In front of a noble suite of tents, which might have served for the Great Mogul, we were received by an insignificant, little, old man, dressed in an old-fashioned military coat, white breeches, sky blue silk stockings, and large glaring buckles to his shoes, having his highly powdered wig, from which depended a pig tail of no ordinary dimensions, surmounted by a

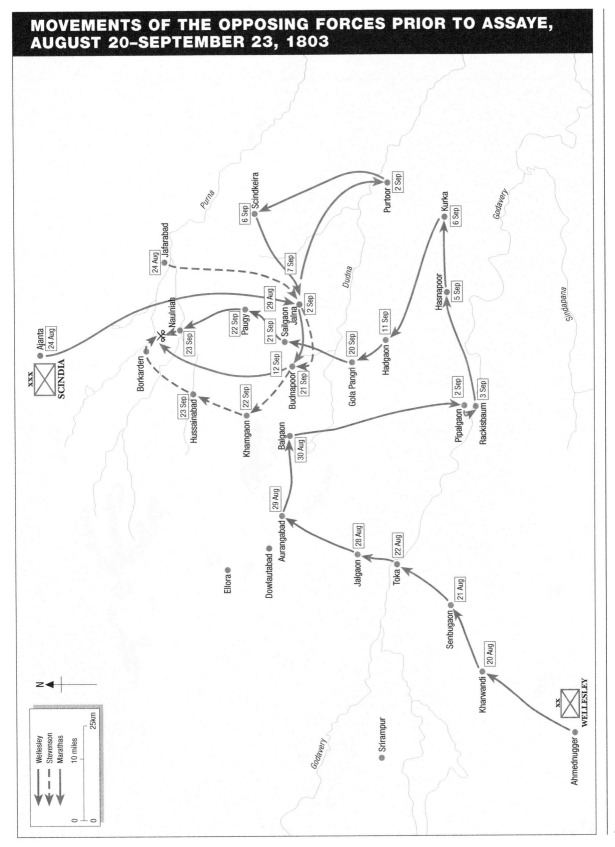

small round black silk hat, ornamented with a single black ostrich feather, looking altogether not unlike a monkey dressed up for Bartholomew fair.

The usual compliments were paid, after which the principals retired into an inner tent. After an indeterminate time they appeared from the tent and Blakiston recollects that he heard Collins telling Wellesley, 'I tell you, General, as to their cavalry, you may ride over them wherever you meet them; but their infantry and guns will astonish you.' Little did they realize how true his words would prove to be.

While in Aurangabad Wellesley was told that Maratha movements had been reported to his south-east. Fearing that they would cross the Godavery, which he now realized was easily forded at any point due to the weak monsoon of 1803, Wellesley, determined to reposition himself between the Marathas and Hyderabad, marched out of Aurangabad at sunrise on August 30 and headed east and then south to the village of Peepalgaon on the Godavery. At the same time he dashed off an instruction to Stevenson to march to Jalna and invest the place. Stevenson arrived at Jalna on September 1 and the next day, having made a breach in the walls with his three iron siege guns, took the place by storm. While Stevenson was capturing Jalna, Wellesley had crossed the river briefly on September 3 and entered Rackisbaum. In Rackisbaum Wellesley learnt from his intelligence system of *hircarrahs* that Scindia had moved from Jalna on August 30 and was at Partoor. Scindia was as well informed as Wellesley and realized that Wellesley was capable of being close on his tail if he was to make a dash for Hyderabad, for although he could march more quickly than the British army, he would never be far enough ahead to be safe or to plunder freely. Scindia decided to remain at Partoor. By September 5 the small British army had re-crossed to the north bank of the Godavery and were at Hasnapur; and a day later at Kurka, the easternmost move; Wellesley had now positioned himself to be on equal terms with the Marathas should they try for Hyderabad. Stevenson had not been idle since capturing Jalna; he anticipated a letter from Wellesley, which arrived on

September 8, urging him to keep the *pindarries* at a great distance and attack them with his cavalry, which had given better than they received in numerous running engagements with the Maratha cavalry. Stevenson had also carried out hit-and-run raids on enemy camps, capturing baggage and cutting off a convoy of enemy provisions on September 9. Meanwhile during the early evening of September 6 Wellesley's *hircarrahs* reported that Scindia had withdrawn northwards towards the Ajanta Hills, no doubt helped on his way by Stevenson's tactics.

As Scindia and Berar were withdrawing northwards they sent orders for the infantry and artillery to move south through the Ajanta Ghaut and join with them. The place at which the concentration of Maratha forces took place was Borkarden. In the meantime, Wellesley was marching north to rendezvous with Stevenson. On September 21 the two British forces were only a few miles apart, Wellesley at Sailgaon and Stevenson at Budnapoor. Wellesley rode over to Colonel Stevenson's camp for a conference to decide the plan of manoeuvre. The *hircarrahs* reported that the Maratha forces around Borkarden consisted of at least two *compoos* of regular infantry battalions and possibly three, with a potential strength in the region of 20,000 trained infantry, 100 organic cannon, and at least 40,000 cavalry. If the Marathas really were camped in the vicinity of Borkarden, Wellesley saw this as the ideal opportunity to finally get to grips with Scindia and Berar, and beat them. The two British commanders agreed upon a simple offensive plan, which would entail their forces remaining separate until uniting on September 24 to give battle. Stevenson was to take the western route marching north-west and then north-east; spend the night of September 23 at Hussainabad; and then march on to Borkarden. Wellesley would take the eastern approach, moving eastwards around the low, flat-topped hills between Budnapoor and Jalna, before turning north and making for Naulniah, where he would spend the night of September 23. They set off in the early hours of the morning of September 22, with Wellesley's column marching 18 miles in six hours to arrive at the village of Paugy around midday, and Stevenson covering a similar distance to camp on the banks of the River Purna at the village of Khamgaon. The *hircarrahs* brought more news of the Marathas: Scindia and Berar were still at Borkarden, they had all their cavalry, and three *compoos* of regular battalions. By this time Wellesley had a good idea of the size and composition of the Maratha units; he would have known that the largest *compoo* was that of a Colonel Pohlmann, consisting of eight battalions, each with a strength of approximately 800, including the artillerymen who manned the four field guns and howitzers per battalion. Pohlmann's cavalry was his weak point, with just 500 men. The second strongest *compoo* was that of the Begum Somroo (but commanded by Colonel Saleur), consisting of five battalions and 25 cannon. This *compoo*, like Pohlmann's, was considered to be of excellent quality. The third *compoo* and weakest, at four battalions, was another of Scindia's, that of Filoze; it was not as well-equipped or commanded, indeed Filoze was not even at Assaye and so the command devolved down to a Dutchman, Major John Dupont. The whole of the regular infantry numbered about 15,000 men, commanded by European officers, with nearly 90 cannon. Scindia and Berar did have in the region of 15,000–20,000 other infantry, but of very dubious quality, certainly not to be trusted in the first line of battle. The Maratha cavalry was vast and although it numbered in the region of 50,000 it was mostly irregular and not suitable for taking part in a pitched battle. Scindia also had a large artillery train that was not part of the *compoos* and these 100-odd guns were exceptionally well made and served. Wellesley's combined force totalled about 15,000 men.

The Godavery River at Rackisbaum. It was seeing the Godavery water levels like this that made Wellesley realize the river was fordable in many places. (Author's photograph)

The track taken by Wellesley's infantry from Naulniah to the village of Peepalgaon, before crossing the Kailna. (Author's photograph)

THE BATTLE OF ASSAYE

As the sun rose again over the eastern horizon on Friday September 23, 1803 and began to bathe the Deccan with its warmth, Wellesley's column set off for the village of Naulniah where he intended to halt for the day – a march of 14 miles. The small army moved with a purpose, knowing that this was no routine march from one place to another; they were marching towards the enemy and knew that a battle was the likely outcome. The Maratha irregular cavalry of Goklah and Appah Dessaye and the light horse of Mysore under Bisnapah were to be seen carrying out their task with more dedication than normal, in advance of the head of the army, gathering information, and screening Wellesley's force from observation by any of Scindia's irregular horse. The order of march for the British army saw Wellesley at the head with the 19 LD and his native cavalry; behind them came the picquets of the day at the head of the six infantry battalions; then the small artillery train, with the extra ammunition in tumbrils; followed by the baggage, the picquets of the previous day, and last of all a squadron of his regular cavalry, bolstered by approximately 800 Mysore horse. The force arrived at Naulniah shortly before 11am, to find the camp had been marked out by the Quartermaster General; Captain Blakiston was surveying the ground, his task on arrival in any new camp. Not long after arriving at Naulniah a patrol of the 19LD brought in two *brinjarries* (grain merchants) who had been intercepted on their way to sell grain in the Maratha camp. Wellesley questioned the two carefully in Hindustani and was told that the camp of Scindia and Berar was not centred solely on

The ford across the Kailna between the villages of Peepalgaon and Waroor. The British infantry crossed in the middle distance. (Author's photograph)

Borkarden, but spread out over a large area to the east for some six miles along the northern bank of the Kailna River, towards a village called Assaye. Clearly there had been an intelligence failure and this undoubtedly came about due to a mistake by Wellesley himself. He had probably relied too heavily on his *hircarrahs* who had travelled with him from Seringapatam; they came from Mysore and it was this fact, not any lack of qualification or ability, that made them a liability when collecting information covertly. Although they spoke Hindustani, they were clearly not from the Deccan and were immediately identifiable as outsiders. This meant that it was very easy for any Maratha sympathizers to feed them disinformation, knowing that it was going to reach Wellesley. To counter this he had started to employ local *hircarrahs*, but the problem was that he did not know them well. In addition, Mountstuart Elphinstone, Wellesley's Marathi interpreter, secretary and EIC senior intelligence officer, although very good at his job, was more comfortable with the Hindustani he had learnt in the north and had trouble communicating in Marathi; as he stated, 'I cannot readily understand all that is said to me, much less say all that I ought to express.'

The news came as a shock to Wellesley, for his plan with Stevenson had been founded on the Maratha camp being around Borkarden. This new development meant that he was five miles closer to the enemy and Stevenson the same distance further away. He had unintentionally encroached too close to the Marathas and the options forming in his head were few. Firstly, he could remain at Naulniah as planned and risk being discovered by Scindia and Berar's *pindarries*, which they surely would be with 18 hours to go before the planned move with Stevenson – and then find no enemy to fight as they would almost certainly have withdrawn further north. Secondly, he could attack now and by achieving surprise catch the Marathas off balance. Wellesley would make no decision until he had carried out his own reconnaissance. He explained to Colonel Maxwell that the escort (19 LD and 4 NC) was to follow him, and that if the enemy did not know he was about it must not be brought to their attention, so they were to remain about half a mile

The British infantry advanced across this ground into the distance to attack the Maratha gun line and infantry behind. (Author's photograph)

to the rear and use dead ground for movement. After giving orders that the camp colours were to be withdrawn and the force to be made ready to advance if ordered, he rode out of the camp with captains Barclay, Campbell, and Blakiston, going in a north-westerly direction. After rising out of the river bed the ground is relatively flat and rolling, with scattered mango trees, scrubby bushes, the odd cactus hedge, and open fields. They rode until about a half a mile from the Kailna River and on cresting a small rise came to a halt in the shade of a mango tree. Wellesley scanned the sight that was before him, and then extending his telescope to its full length, did a detailed survey of the Maratha lines. He saw Scindia's European-officered infantry and artillery, who were bivouacked on the left of the Maratha camp, in a well-ordered manner stretching for nearly two miles between the villages of Kodully and Taunklee. To their right he saw a mass of Maratha cavalry, who were not nearly so orderly. The Marathas were breaking camp and planning to either fight or more likely move off. After a while some Maratha cavalry started to cross the Kailna at Kodully; Wellesley and his party rode on for approximately three miles to the east, where he stopped again for another survey. From this vantage point he saw Scindia's regular battalions, with their cannon to the front, beginning to form up on some high ground to the north of the Kailna River. He would also have seen that the mass of Maratha cavalry was still on the right of the infantry. Wellesley decided to attack and chose the Maratha left flank as his point of contact. The Marathas, however, were perfectly aware that he was in the vicinity, and were also aware of the position of Colonel Stevenson. Scindia and Berar and the rest of their advisers were convinced that Wellesley would not attack with such small numbers; the sensible step would be to join forces with Stevenson. They also reasoned that it would suit their purpose to see the two British forces combined and then defeat them in a single battle. The Marathas committed the cardinal sin of deciding the enemy plan and basing their plan on that. What they did not appreciate was that Arthur Wellesley had a belief in offensive action, particularly when the odds were stacked against him, and that he held no fear of failure.

CROSSING THE KAILNA

Wellesley set his plan in motion, and orders were sent back to Naulniah. The baggage train was to remain at Naulniah with the 1/2 MNI as the guard force. The remainder of the infantry would march north via Barahjala in the following order of march: picquets of the day, 74th Foot, 2/12 MNI, 1/4 MNI, 1/8 MNI, 1/10 MNI, and lastly the 78th Foot. The battalion guns were to march parallel to the infantry. Maxwell with all the cavalry was initially to provide a screen to the north-west, but south of the Kailna River to protect the advancing column from interference by the irregular Maratha cavalry.

The crossing point chosen by Wellesley was quite logical. He could not afford to attack the Maratha position frontally; he was simply not strong enough and it was the wrong option anyway. He also realized that he needed to defeat the Maratha regular battalions to make plain to Scindia's forces that British arms were superior. This meant that in true Frederick the Great fashion he had to turn their left flank to catch them in the flank, or if they re-deployed, to strike them when off balance. The crossing point therefore dictated itself, and after initially being told that no such point existed between Peepalgaon and Waroor on the Kailna, he made the decision to cross there anyway. He had been in India long enough and conducted sufficient river crossings to know that there was almost certainly a ford between the two villages; and so it was to prove.

Wellesley had been riding Diomed, his Arab horse, during the reconnaissance and he now changed to a classic English bay hunter before riding to the head of the infantry column. Blakiston describes how they felt:

> Not a whisper was heard through the ranks; our nerves were wound up to the proper pitch, and every one seemed to know and feel that there was no alternative but death or victory.

Wellesley realized that the success of the operation was dependent on there being a ford where he anticipated one. As his force neared the river he urged his horse into a canter for the last few hundred yards and was

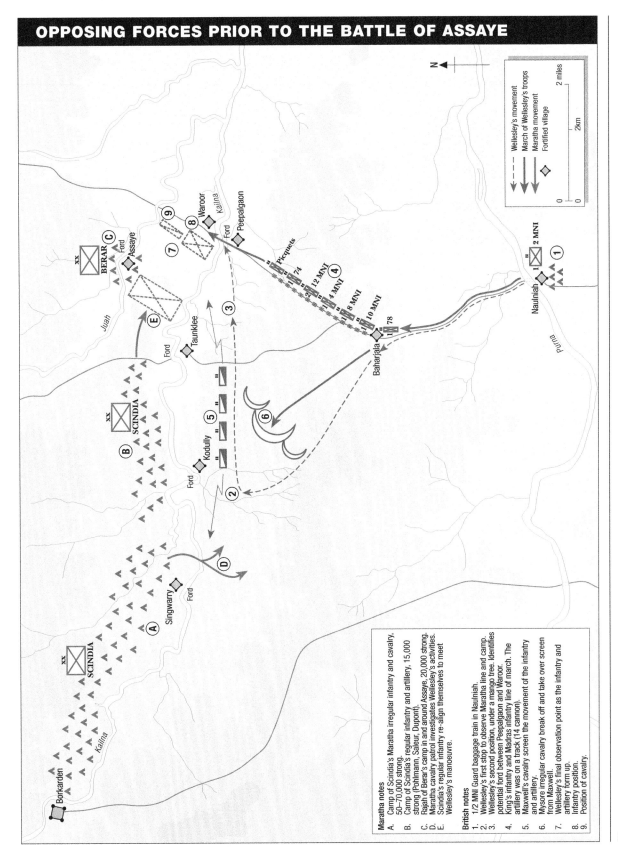

Maratha notes

A. Camp of Scindia's Maratha irregular infantry and cavalry, 50–70,000 strong.
B. Camp of Scindia's regular infantry and artillery, 15,000 strong (Pohlmann, Saleur, Dupont).
C. Rajah of Berar's camp in and around Assaye, 20,000 strong.
D. Maratha cavalry patrol investigates Wellesley's activities.
E. Scindia's regular infantry re-align themselves to meet Wellesley's manoeuvre.

British notes

1. 1/2 MNI Guard baggage train in Naulniah.
2. Wellesley's first stop to observe Maratha line and camp.
3. Wellesley's second position, under a mango tree. Identifies potential ford between Peepalgaon and Waroor.
4. King's infantry and Madras infantry line of march. The artillery was on a track (14 cannon).
5. Maxwell's cavalry screen the movement of the infantry and artillery.
6. Mysore irregular cavalry break off and take over screen from Maxwell.
7. Wellesley's final observation point as the infantry and artillery form up.
8. Infantry position.
9. Position of cavalry.

the first into the water, no doubt breathing a sigh of relief when discovering the water was less than three feet deep. The Marathas, however, were not going to let the British cross the river unhindered, and soon started up a long-range fire. The range was too great to offer anything other than harassing fire, with the secondary effect of slowing the British down, but this did allow Scindia's infantry to change their formation to meet the threat that was developing on their left flank. The Maratha gunners were only able to lob round shot in the direction of the ford, as they were unable to see the fall of shot properly due to the undulating ground, the clefts in the river bank, and the distance. Wellesley left Captain Campbell to supervise the river crossing while he went on ahead with Captain Barclay to look at the ground for the forming up. Some of the first cannon shot found their mark as the head of the infantry column reached the far bank; men ducked as a ball went rebounding over their heads, only to look up as Captain Campbell was thrown from his horse, which had been hit in the leg. A few moments later Wellesley's dragoon orderly had the top of his head carried off by a

One of the few remaining sections of the wall that surrounded Assaye in 1803. (Rupert Millar)

cannon shot; the gruesome incident did not end there as his body was kept in the saddle by his holsters and valise and it was a few minutes before the terrified horse, kicking and plunging, was able to rid itself of the horrible burden. Blakiston was then called forward by Wellesley to examine the ground in the direction of the enemy; on putting his horse into a gallop a fox rose up in front of him and 'with a swing of his brush dashed off towards the Marathas'. His route went very close to the enemy vedettes and it was lucky for Blakiston that they seemed too intent on their own business to meddle with him, as he had left his weapons with his groom. With the infantry crossing the river Wellesley sent word to Colonel Maxwell for him to bring in the regular cavalry and form up on the right rear of the infantry, but to leave the Mysore and Maratha irregular cavalry to carry out his task on the south bank.

By the time Blakiston returned with his report the infantry were across the river and had formed up in column in two lines running south to north. The first line had (from left to right) the 78th Foot, 1/10 MNI, 1/8 MNI and the picquets; the second had 1/4 MNI, 2/12 MNI, and the 74th Foot. Blakiston reported to Wellesley that Scindia's battalions had changed their front and taken up a new position, with their left on the village of Assaye and their right on the Kailna River. Wellesley's own reconnaissance had shown him that Assaye was very heavily defended and had to be avoided. He immediately changed his order of battle, realizing that he had to extend his front to meet the new threat that the Maratha line posed. He rode over to give orders to each of the battalion commanders personally. The infantry was to attack in a single line, which would require Lieutenant-Colonel Orrock, commanding the picquets, to move obliquely to his right, leaving enough space for two MNI battalions on his left; but he was to keep away from Assaye and was instructed that the 74th Foot would form up on his right flank. Wellesley then rode over to Major Swinton, in temporary command of the 74th Foot; they were to follow the picquets until they formed into line, when he was to double the 74th forward and take the right of the line; again, Wellesley emphasized staying clear of Assaye. The 2/12 MNI and 1/4 MNI were his next port of call. He told both commanding officers to march obliquely to the north in column and then form into line to the right of the 1/8 MNI in the gap left by Orrock. He

WELLESLEY RECONNOITRES THE MARATHA CAMP WITH HIS STAFF (pages 58–59)

Major-General Arthur Wellesley carries out his reconnaissance of the Maratha camp on the Kailna River at approximately midday on September 23, 1803. Wellesley was surprised to learn on arriving in Naulniah that the Maratha encampment was as close as it was. Like any good commander he immediately went to see for himself the extent of his problem. A good stable of horses was an important asset for any commander, particularly a man like Wellesley, who was capable of riding upwards of 40 miles a day, therefore needing frequent changes. Diomed (1) his favourite horse, was an Arab; he had originally belonged to Colonel Ashton, a friend of Wellesley's, who bequeathed him to Wellesley as he lay dying from a duelling wound. With his fitness and agility, Diomed got Wellesley out of numerous tight spots in India, only to die from a pike wound at Assaye. Generals need staff officers to help them carry out the planning and co-ordination of their army's operation; Wellesley was no different. Captain William Barclay (2) was an officer who had gained Wellesley's confidence in the campaign against Doondiah Waugh in 1800. He was a very competent EIC officer who hailed from the Shetland Islands and had the responsibilities of adjutant-general. Lieutenant-Colonel Patrick Maxwell of the 19th Light Dragoons (3) commanded Wellesley's cavalry during the campaign. He was well-liked and a valiant officer, who led his men with a light cavalry dash, but was killed in the final charge at

Assaye. The light cavalry horse (4) was only slightly smaller than the heavy cavalry counterpart, with the majority in a regiment being 15 hands. Officers had to purchase their own horses; troop commanders were allowed two or three, whereas Maxwell would have had four horses. If officers could afford it they would buy English hunters, famed for their stamina and fleetness of foot. The colours of the horses ridden were brown, bay and chestnut, with trumpeters riding greys. At the Battle of Laswaree (November 1, 1803) the entire regiment of the 8th Light Dragoons was mounted on greys, the property of the King of Oudh, except their commanding officer, Thomas Vandeleur, who rode his own black racehorse. Lieutenant John Blakiston (5) was an engineer officer. Like all engineer officers he was trained at Woolwich, which he left in 1801 aged 17. Blakiston arrived in India in 1802 to take up his appointment on the EIC Madras Establishment. He accompanied Wellesley throughout the Deccan campaign and was at all the major engagements. His further exploits included blowing up the inner gate at Vellore in 1806 (Vellore Mutiny). He remained in India till 1811, before starting on his last military adventures as a captain in a Portuguese infantry regiment during the Peninsular War. The escort for the reconnaissance was provided by the 19th Light Dragoons and the 4th Native Cavalry (6). The 4th Native Cavalry became the Light Cavalry in 1819 and in 1876 The Prince of Wales' Madras Light Cavalry. Royal connections, however, did not save them from disbandment in 1891. (Peter Dennis)

finally visited the 1/8 MNI and 1/10 MNI and gave them orders to form from column into line and move forward and take up positions on the right flank of the 78th Foot. This meant that the British line would advance in the oblique order, and so Wellesley positioned himself with the 78th Foot, as they were likely to be in contact first.

While Wellesley had been dashing about issuing new orders, the Maratha artillery had opened up a well-directed fire on the British infantry. When at last some of the British artillery had crossed the Kailna, they started to return fire on the Maratha gun line. Soon the Maratha guns were engaging the British gun line in counter-battery fire, which was an unequal affair, with the British guns not only being out-numbered but also outgunned, with their 6-pdrs against the Maratha 9- and 12-pdr guns. The Maratha cannon wreaked havoc on the British gun line, smashing artillery carriages, killing their crews, and knocking down bullocks with almost every shot. At the same time the British infantry were receiving severe casualties as the Maratha shot bounded through the artillery and into their lines, and as chain shot came whirring towards them, bent on causing carnage. Time was becoming critical, for if the British infantry remained where they stood they would be destroyed by the Maratha artillery. Wellesley knew that he had to regain momentum and the initiative, and force the Maratha line to respond to his infantry advancing. The order was given for the infantry guns to be left behind and for the infantry to advance.

THE ADVANCE TO CLOSE WITH THE ENEMY

The British infantry had been standing patiently, with their muskets 'at the order', waiting for the word to come to advance. Those in the ranks knew it would be soon, for the order to fix bayonets was given; with a flash of metal, 5,000 bayonets left their scabbards and were whipped around to the front, placed against the musket barrels, and made secure. With the next order to 'shoulder firelock' given they were ready. The command 'forward' rang out, and with a cheer, the red-coated infantry started their advance, with the battalions forming line from column as ordered with cool precision. As the line advanced the sun occasionally broke through the smoke of battle and glinted off the accoutrements and bayonets; soon the advancing infantry were able to make out the near continuous line of Maratha infantry running from Assaye to the Kailna River. Far more forbidding was the line of Maratha artillery, seemingly wheel to wheel in front of their infantry and with the Maratha gunners working them to the maximum rate in professional manner. Wellesley was unaware that the Maratha leadership would not command their forces at the battle. Berar had long gone, taking his women with him. Scindia was far out of range at the other end of the encampment, and was soon to depart; the Hanoverian adventurer Colonel Pohlmann was in command.

All was not well with the British advance, however. While the 78th Foot and the four MNI battalions had successfully carried out their orders to form line and advance towards the Maratha line, Orrock was

The Juah River course. The British cavalry chased the Maratha horsemen and some of their infantry over the Juah River after the first successful charge. (Author's photograph)

Wellesley on Diomed watches as a King's battalion contacts the enemy. Although engraved in 1816, the dress of the King's regiment is incorrect as it can only be the 78th Foot. (ASKB)

leading the picquets in the wrong direction, obliquely and directly towards the village of Assaye. Behind him Major Swinton with the 74th Foot was dutifully obeying orders to follow the picquets and form on their right when they straightened up; the 74th Foot was heading towards destruction. Wellesley at this time did not realize that his line had split into two main actions.

The attack in the southern sector was delivered slightly en echelon from left to right. The soldiers of the 78th Foot, with Wellesley riding close to their right flank, were the first to come into action. The kilted Highlanders made for an impressive sight as they advanced at a steady pace before halting about 50 yards from the Maratha gun line. On the command 'present ... fire', a volley was unleashed at the Maratha gunners; after recovering and reloading, the line once again moved off

INITIAL BATTLE MOVEMENTS AT ASSAYE

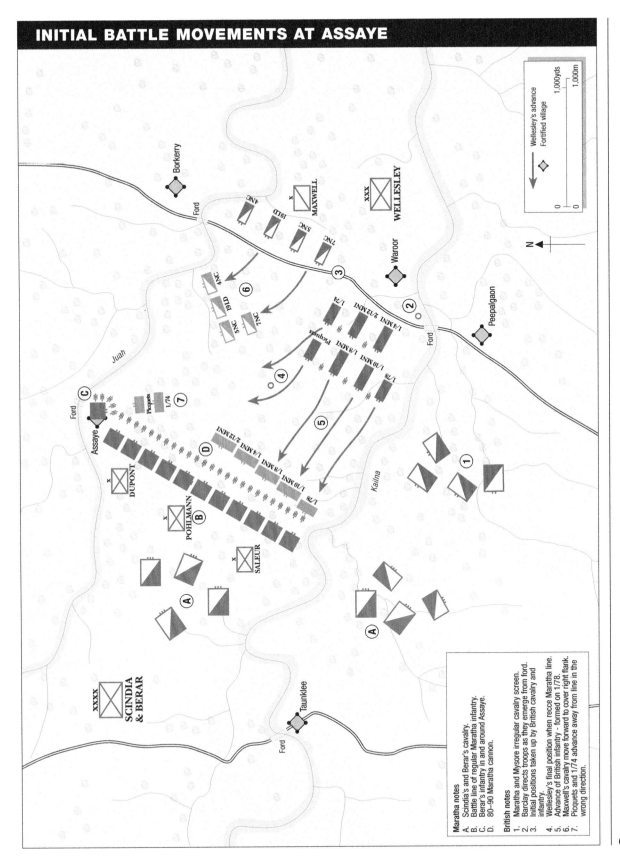

Maratha notes
- A. Scindia's and Berar's cavalry.
- B. Battle line of regular Maratha infantry.
- C. Berar's infantry in and around Assaye.
- D. 80–90 Maratha cannon.

British notes
1. Maratha and Mysore irregular cavalry screen.
2. Barclay directs troops as they emerge from ford.
3. Initial positions taken up by British cavalry and infantry.
4. Wellesley's final position when recce Maratha line.
5. Advance of British infantry – formed on 1/78.
6. Maxwell's cavalry move forward to cover right flank.
7. Picquets and 1/74 advance away from line in the wrong direction.

A glorious depiction of the British infantry attacking the Maratha line. Sadly, the image is largely inaccurate. (Mary Evans Picture Library)

The Bombay Artillery provided fire support to the British army. The descendants of this battery are today's 10th (Assaye Battery) Royal Artillery. (David Rowlands)

and drove through the gun line, attacking the gunners with their bayonets. Some of the gunners continued to work their guns; others had managed to duck under them and struck out at the passing Redcoats with their Maratha spears and Rajput half-pikes. Following the example of the 78th Foot, the 1/10 MNI halted and fired a volley as they too came up to within 50 yards of the Maratha gun line; they then reloaded and pressed home the attack, dealing with the gunners in a similar fashion. The 1/8 MNI, 1/4 MNI, and the 2/12 MNI all carried out the same manoeuvres, perfectly sequenced for time and space and with the same devastating effect.

Scindia's regular infantrymen were good soldiers and probably the best sepoys in India after the East India Company battalions, but their morale was now shaken. The red-coated infantry had brushed aside the feared Maratha artillery and were now bearing down on them. Again the British infantry halted, and from the 78th Foot to the 2/12 MNI in sequence fired a second volley, this time at the Maratha infantry, before

The Maratha line recoils from the charge of a King's regiment. This picture, engraved in 1816, once again features many inaccuracies; however, the action is beautifully drawn. (Author's collection)

reloading and continuing the advance. It became all too much for the last two battalions on the right of Pohlmann's line, which broke, causing the southern half of the line to give way. The Maratha infantry withdrew towards their secondary position, a line, with the left flank on Assaye, running east-west along the southern bank of the Juah River. The officers of the MNI battalions temporarily lost control as, encouraged by their success, the sepoys pursued the Marathas as they tried to escape, slaughtering many in the process. Seeing the disordered sepoys, the 20,000 Maratha cavalry still on the north bank of the Kailna made as if to charge into the mêlée. However, this moment of danger passed for the British; the 78th Foot had not been carried away in the pursuit, but had re-formed into column of companies and presented a confident front to the Maratha horsemen who shied away from any action. The two Bombay 6-pdrs assigned to the 78th Foot had managed to reach the British line to give fire support, and they now opened up on the Maratha cavalry, completing their discomfiture. The discipline of the 78th Foot and the arrival of the Bombay gunners gave the MNI officers time to rally and steady their excited men.

While the attack had been going in Wellesley had been giving encouragement to the 78th Foot and 1/10 MNI, and when near the Maratha gun line his fine bay horse had been shot from under him. He avoided being trapped underneath by nimbly springing from the animal and had only a short time to wait until his groom brought up Diomed. Once in the saddle again, he gave orders to the 78th Foot on his left and the MNI on his right to remain in position and to be prepared to follow up the Maratha infantry. Having done this, he became aware of and heard gun fire from the direction of Assaye. Fearing the worst he rode swiftly north over ground littered with Maratha and British casualties from the assault on Pohlmann's line. Everything was well in this sector, as all the battalions had successfully carried out their attack.

The picquets and 74th Foot, however, were in serious trouble. Orrock had made a mistake that happens all too often in war, by either not understanding his orders or becoming confused in the heat of

THE BRITISH ATTACK ON THE MARATHA INFANTRY
(pages 66–67)

The 1/8th Madras Native Infantry advance towards the Maratha line. The native infantry were the mainstay of British armies in India and if it had not been for their loyalty and professionalism it is unlikely that British arms would have prevailed, particularly in the early years before the Raj. In the days of the East India Company, infantry companies in native regiments were commanded by either British or Indian officers (1). The rank structure for native officers was the same as for their British counterparts, but with different names: a *subedar* was a captain and a *jemadar* a lieutenant. When a British officer was away from his company one of his Indian *jemadars* would take command and so it was not unusual to find five or six companies being commanded by native officers on campaign. In common with British infantry of the time, the native infantry regiments carried regimental colours (2), which were treated with the same reverence. A sepoy on enlistment swore his oath in front of the colours and during the oath he swore 'to serve the Honourable Company ... against all their enemies ... while I continue ... to eat their salt ... and never abandon my Colours'. The eating of salt appealed to a man's personal honour and the oath bound his fidelity to a visible symbol, the colours. The 1/8 MNI (3) were originally raised as the 9th Battalion Coast Sepoys in 1760, becoming the 1/8th Madras Native Infantry in 1796. They retained the title of 8th Madras Native/Madras Infantry until 1902 when they became the 8th Gurkhas and were also disbanded. During the years that Wellesley was in India they took to calling themselves 'Wellesley's Own'. Of the other MNI at Assaye, the 1/10 eventually became the 10th Gurkha Rifles; the 1/4 the 2nd Battalion Madras Pioneers; and the 2/12 the 10th Battalion 1st Punjab Regiment. The 1/2, who remained at Naulniah, went on to become the 1st Battalion, 1st Punjab Regiment. One of the roles of a commander in battle was to give encouragement to his troops (4). Wellesley was a master at being in the right place at the right time, and it was this ability that gave his troops confidence in the plan and in him as their commander. For a commander to be seen in the thick of battle was a great boost for his men, but he had to temper his direct involvement with remaining in control of events elsewhere on the field. Elephants (5) due to their strength and intelligence were unbeatable when used as draught animals; they were used for pulling artillery pieces, particularly the large siege guns, and pontoon trains. The drawback was the cost of maintaining them, for each one consumed daily 40 lb. of rice, 1 lb. ghee (clarified butter), 1 lb. date palm juice, and 40 coconut palm leaves or equivalent. Elephants were also used for recreational purposes even on campaign, and many an officer went shooting tigers to relieve periods of boredom. (Peter Dennis)

battle, or both. Instead of inclining to the right and leaving a gap for the MNI battalions to fill in, he had continued north in column towards the village of Assaye, which was garrisoned by upwards of 20,000 infantry and 40 cannon. The 74th Foot had followed as ordered, but had probably formed line in anticipation of the picquets wheeling as planned. The wayward British units soon found themselves engulfed by a maelstrom of fire, with the Maratha artillery, not being assaulted by Wellesley's attack, and those around Assaye pouring fire into them. Soon the picquets had been all but destroyed, with the survivors falling back on the 74th Foot, who had reached a cactus hedge. The 74th Foot recoiled too for about 150 yards and were soon being attacked by Maratha cavalry and some of the infantry battalions of Pohlmann's line closest to Assaye. The gallant survivors of the picquets and the 74th Foot formed a square of sorts and repelled the attack, which milled about them on all sides. Sergeant Swarbruck of the 19 LD had a grandstand view of the carnage, while waiting to receive orders: 'the enemy then charged our infantry on the retreat … gave no quarter to any of our wounded'. The rough square stood firm and defiant in the face of the onslaught. As Wellesley was riding up to see what had happened to Orrock, he ordered his cavalry commander, Maxwell, to bring the 19 LD, 4 NC, and 5 NC forward to the extreme right of what had become the second line.

THE FIRST CAVALRY CHARGE

Wellesley rode up to Maxwell and gave the orders to charge, 'or we shall be done'. With a loud cheer the 19 LD, 4 NC, and 5 NC dashed forward straight for the carnage that was the remnants of the picquets and the 74th Foot. The milling mass of Maratha cavalry and infantry was taken by surprise as the disciplined British cavalry, on bigger and stronger horses, crashed into them. The fight was short and violent as the British troopers, with their hours of sword exercise, cut and thrust their way through the Maratha cavalry, clearing the area around the ravaged British infantry. Maxwell's cavalry now had the enemy cannon around Assaye in their

This early painting by Simkin shows a rather fanciful view of the 19th Light Dragoons' charge. (ASKB)

OPPOSITE **The 74th Foot, inaccurately drawn with feather bonnets, are caught falling back by the Maratha cavalry. (ASKB)**

BELOW **The 74th Foot, having formed line, advance into the maelstrom that was around Assaye. The moment shown is just before the 74th had to fall back and form a square. (David Rowlands)**

Maratha cavalry cut down some of the 74th Foot that had not made it back to the square. (ASKB)

Major Swinton, commanding the 74th Foot at Assaye, rallies his men to form a square and fight off the Maratha cavalry. (Pen and ink by David Rowlands/private collection)

sights and were soon galloping on to deal with them. The Maratha gunners, however, did not flee, realizing that to stay with their guns was the key to survival as they would be doomed if caught fleeing in the open. When the British cavalry arrived at the gun line the gunners were waiting for them and a fierce mêlée developed amongst the Maratha cannon. While trying to cut down a gunner, one horseman, Lieutenant Grant, acting as Maxwell's brigade major, got his horse wedged between the barrel and a wheel just as the gun discharged. Captain Sale of the 19 LD found himself in a tricky position, for, while attempting to deal with a Maratha gunner wielding a half-pike or spear, another gunner climbed atop the cannon and thrust his weapon at Sale. The captain received a cut across his sternum and was relieved to be helped by Sergeant Strange of his regiment, who, seeing his predicament, rode to his rescue and ran the Maratha through with his sword. However, as he leant out of the saddle to deal with his quarry, an unseen Maratha gunner, sheltering under the cannon, thrust a spear upwards into his abdomen. Scenes like this were repeated elsewhere, but soon the Marathas were driven from the gun line, as were some of the infantry behind them. The mass of infantry, cavalry and artillery gunner refugees were driven down the river bank and across the Juah River with great slaughter, with the British cavalry splashing their way across the river and onto the northern bank, determined to press home their advantage. Command and control of the British cavalry had broken down and they were in danger of being cut off by some irregular Maratha horse waiting further up the north bank. Luckily for the British cavalry the Maratha horsemen were not trained or used for direct charges against well-armed European cavalry. Their role was to harass convoys, foraging parties, and the like. Maxwell now started to rally his horsemen on the north bank and as the bugle calls rang out the British cavalry began to re-form; soon they were once again splashing their way through the Juah River to take up a position on the south bank to the east of Assaye.

RESTORATION OF CONTROL IN THE CENTRE

No sooner was the right flank under control than Wellesley had to restore order in the central sector of the battlefield. The British infantry found themselves being fired upon by the very guns that they had recently overrun and by the Maratha infantry, which had momentarily stopped withdrawing. Maratha gunners left for dead by the first infantry assault had remanned some of their guns, turned them 180 degrees, and started firing on the backs of the re-formed British infantry. The act of feigning death was considered to be less than chivalric by many of the British officers. Wellesley immediately assessed the situation and issued clear instructions. The four MNI battalions, having re-formed, were to use two battalions to watch the Maratha irregular cavalry on their left flank and the remaining two sepoy battalions were to continue to face the re-forming Maratha infantry; the 78th Foot were to retake the Maratha artillery line for the second time, this time from the west. He then rode to where the 7 NC stood. The 7 NC was the one regiment which had not been involved in Maxwell's first charge and were still relatively fresh. Wellesley led them against the Maratha gun line from the east. The fighting around the guns was once again a short and bloody affair; the Maratha gunners defended their guns fiercely, using spears and Rajput half-pikes, but were soon driven off by the bayonets and sabres of the 78th Foot and the 7 NC. Wellesley had been in the thick of the fighting, almost certainly having to use his own sword, and it was during this attack that his favourite charger Diomed was piked under him. The saddle and pistol holsters were moved to another horse and Wellesley mounted his third horse of the day and issued new instructions. The 7 NC with all the cavalry galloper guns were to remain on the recaptured Maratha gun line, with

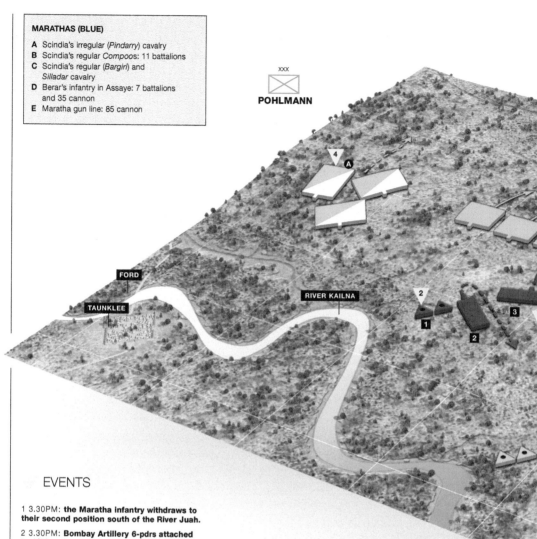

MARATHAS (BLUE)

A Scindia's irregular (*Pindarry*) cavalry
B Scindia's regular *Compoos*: 11 battalions
C Scindia's regular (*Bargiri*) and *Silladar* cavalry
D Berar's infantry in Assaye: 7 battalions and 35 cannon
E Maratha gun line: 85 cannon

xxx

POHLMANN

RIVER JUAH

FORD

TAUNKLEE

RIVER KAILNA

EVENTS

1 3.30PM: **the Maratha infantry withdraws to their second position south of the River Juah.**

2 3.30PM: **Bombay Artillery 6-pdrs attached to 1/78 arrive and open up on the Maratha cavalry. 1/78 reformed in column of quarter companies.**

3 3.30PM: **1/74 and picquets continue to come under a withering fire from Scindia's Maratha infantry and artillery, and Berar's artillery ringing Assaye.**

4 3.40PM: **Maratha *Pindarry* cavalry move off and head north of the River Juah.**

5 3.40–3.45PM: **British Madras Native Infantry battalions reform.**

6 3.45PM: **Maratha gunners re-man some of their guns and start firing at the British infantry.**

7 4.00PM: **Maratha *Bargiri* and *Silladar* cavalry attack the remnants of the picquets and 1/74 (in a square).**

8 4.10PM: **British cavalry under Colonel Maxwell carry out their first charge against the Maratha line and push the Maratha cavalry across the River Juah.**

9 4.20PM: **the British cavalry over-enthusiastically chase the Marathas to the north bank, and have to rally.**

10 4.30PM: **Wellesley orders the 1/78 and 7 MNC to recapture the Maratha gun line. Wellesley is riding Diomed, who is piked and killed at the gun line.**

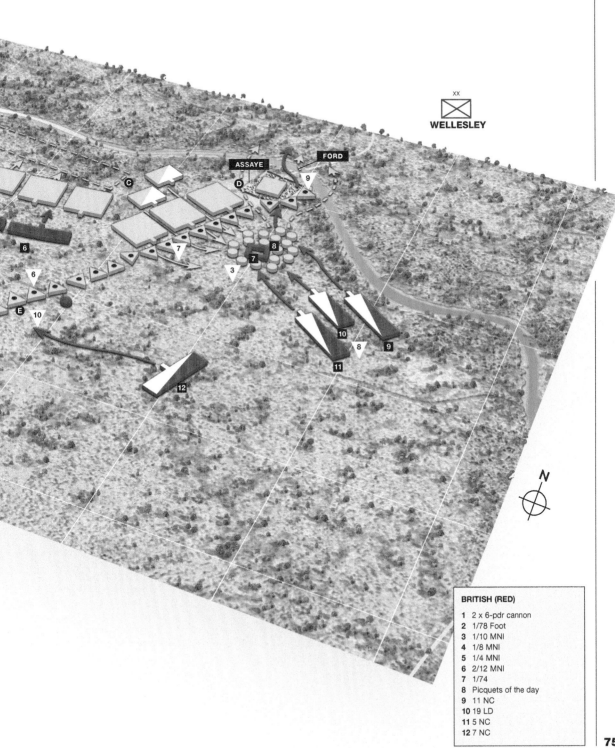

WELLESLEY

ASSAYE

FORD

BRITISH (RED)

1 2 x 6-pdr cannon
2 1/78 Foot
3 1/10 MNI
4 1/8 MNI
5 1/4 MNI
6 2/12 MNI
7 1/74
8 Picquets of the day
9 11 NC
10 19 LD
11 5 NC
12 7 NC

The Maratha horsemen charge through the smoke to try to destroy the remnants of the picquets and the 74th Foot. (Author's collection)

The 19th Light Dragoons engage in a mêlée with the Maratha horse. (The Highlanders Regimental Museum)

Captain Sale (on the right) engages in a melee with some Maratha artillerymen. Sergeant Strange (left) comes to help, but is speared by a Maratha under the cannon. Although both were wounded, they survived. (Pen and ink by David Rowlands/ private collection)

two tasks: firstly, to provide rear-area security, and secondly, to ensure the recaptured enemy guns were not carried off by the Marathas. Orders were then sent to Harness that he was to re-form the infantry into the same order of battle as for the first assault on the Maratha line and be prepared to attack them. The 78th Foot rejoined the left flank of the infantry line. He then rode north once again to see Maxwell.

THE FINAL INFANTRY ADVANCE AND MAXWELL'S DEATH RIDE

Wellesley was delighted to see Maxwell re-forming his three regiments and issued new orders that he was to charge the left flank of Pohlmann's new line. Pohlmann was an above-average commander, and while Maxwell's first cavalry charge was taking place and Wellesley was restoring the centre, he spent his time re-forming his line. The left flank was now anchored on the village of Assaye, with the remains of the infantry in a line stretching back for approximately a mile along the Juah. This position was relatively strong and at least three of Pohlmann's infantry battalions had not been engaged; his only problem was that he could call on no more than 15 cannon.

Wellesley's plan was to advance the British infantry against the new Maratha line from the south as Maxwell charged the line from the east. Maxwell's cavalry had been reduced to 600 effective sabres; they had reformed with the 'French blue' jackets of the 19 LD in the centre, with the red coats of the 4 and 5 NC on either flank. Maxwell's trumpeter signalled for the advance to begin, their harnesses jingling as they moved into the walk, followed by the trot and then the canter. The cavalry made a splendid sight as they advanced against the Maratha line; however, they were making their attack from an angle of 45 degrees and not 90. As the troopers heard

Having charged through the mêlée around the 74th's square, the 19th Light Dragoons scattered some of the Maratha infantry, pushing them back into the Juah. (David Rowlands)

the trumpet call for the charge they were met with a shower of canister and musquetry from the Maratha line, which rattled through the ranks of the cavalry and claimed the life of their commander. Maxwell was pierced in the body by several pieces of canister, with one piece striking his right hand or arm in such a violent manner that the arm shot up into the air, as he dropped his sword and slid to the ground. Those following thought they had seen the signal for the halt and tried to rein in the charge. Blakiston describes what happened next; wanting to be part of a cavalry charge, he had borrowed a sword from Wellesley's orderly and joined the ranks of the 19 LD:

I suddenly found my horse swept round as it were by an eddy torrent. Away we galloped, right shoulders forward, along the whole of the enemy's line, receiving their fire as we passed, till, having turned our

RIGHT **The 7th Native Cavalry advance to retake the Maratha gun line. (Pen and ink by David Rowlands/private collection)**

LEFT **In the centre, the Maratha gunners, some having feigned death, turn their guns on the British infantry who have re-formed beyond them. (Author's collection)**

Wellesley dismounts from Diomed who bleeds from a pike wound. Native cavalry can be seen charging in the rear. (ASKB)

backs upon them, we took to our heels manfully, every one calling out, "Halt! halt!" while nobody would set the example; till at last, a trumpet sounded, we pulled up, but in complete disorder, dragoons and native cavalry pell-mell.

Meanwhile Wellesley had once again taken up a position to the right of the 78th Foot and was going forward with the infantry line. The battalions were once again advancing en echelon from the left to deal with Pohlmann's new line. Although tired, the British line advanced with a steady and

Another depiction of Wellesley leading the recovery of the Maratha gun line. Diomed is about to be piked. (ASKB)

Lieutenant-Colonel Maxwell of the 19th Light Dragoons is killed leading the second charge against the left of the re-formed Maratha line. (Mary Evans Picture Library)

menacing purpose towards the Maratha infantry; the Marathas in turn watched and waited as the resolute red-coated infantry came on, remembering how previously they had been unceremoniously pushed off their first position. Soon a general feeling of uneasiness permeated the Maratha ranks; the desire to face up to the volley that was sure to come, followed by the bayonet attack, was not there. Some say that the Marathas, on Pohlmann's command, turned to their right and marched off quickly, abandoning their cannon as they moved across the Juah River; others that the line melted away without receiving word to do so. Whatever the circumstances, the Maratha infantry left the field of battle in the hands of the British infantry.

The village of Assaye was the last remaining hub of resistance and Wellesley now organized the attack on the village. He immediately ordered the two 6-pdrs of the 78th Foot, some of the MNI battalion guns, and half the cavalry gallopers to advance within 300 yards of Assaye. They fired a few rounds at the village, but as it turned out the village was no longer a threat. The guns that had caused such devastation earlier were silent, while the garrison of Berar's men, having seen the fate of the best of Scindia's infantry, decided enough was enough. Two British battalions took the village of Assaye with little difficulty; by the time they advanced, the majority of Berar's infantry had left the village and were on the north side of the Juah River and marching off.

From the south bank the British soldiers watched the Marathas march off. Then, tired and dusty, they knelt and quenched their thirst from the river; the Battle of Assaye was over.

THE AFTERMATH OF THE BATTLE

The British army was too exhausted from their long approach march and then the battle to follow up the Marathas effectively. Wellesley did send some of the 7 NC in pursuit, but this was half-hearted at best. As the sun set on the battlefield they settled down to rest as best they could amongst the carnage of battle. Blakiston recalls his actions:

As to myself, I lay down with my horse's bridle in my hand, close to an officer of the 74th, who had lost his leg. He appeared in good spirits considering his situation and was so kind as to offer me a share of some brandy which his servant had brought up. In the morning I turned around to repeat my thanks for his kindness, and to inquire after his wound. He was a corpse!

Wellesley spent the night on some straw in a farmyard, as tired as the next man, but with many more problems to be resolved the next day. Some of the Marathas spent the night only 12 miles from the battlefield; many, though, did not pass the night so quietly, for seized with panic they did not stop until they were safe at the bottom of the Ajanta Ghaut, which at the time represented a rough border between the Marathas' and Nizam's territories.

The British casualties have been assessed as being in the region of 428 killed, 1,138 wounded, and 18 missing – a total of 1,584, suggesting that Wellesley's force suffered in the region of 35 per cent casualties.

Asseerghur. The capture of Asseerghur by Colonel Stevenson gave Wellesley another fortress at which to base his operations if necessary, and a new supply centre, this time in the north. (British Library/India Office)

There were no returns rendered for Maratha casualties but these were estimated at around 6,000. The task of sorting out the casualties took a long time, with British officers up to four days later still trying to account for their men and decide whom should be sent back to the field hospital once established. Captain Welsh, who was not at the battle but passed over the battlefield when marching to rejoin the army later, wrote:

The battle of Assaye had collected all the birds of prey in the country, a few following the army, and the rest taking possession of the inheritance left them, by their kindest benefactor man, on the field of battle.

Stevenson arrived at Assaye during the early evening of September 24. On September 25, 36 hours after the battle, the British pursuit of Scindia began again in earnest, when Stevenson with his army, less the surgeons, marched for the Ajanta Ghaut. As they marched north, they were met with the sight of the roads littered with the bodies of dead men and animals; they also recovered four brass field guns abandoned at the bottom of the Ajanta Ghaut. Wellesley's main concern was to reconstitute his force as a fighting machine. The sepoy battalions had suffered insufficient casualties to render them ineffective, but still Wellesley recalled the 1/3 MNI, Captain Welsh's regiment, to the army from its garrison duties in Poona. The next step was to ask the *killadar* of the Dowlautabad fort near Aurangabad if the fort could be used as a hospital. By putting the wounded into a fortified position, it would mean that he did not have to worry about providing a large guard for them. His request was refused and the wounded and their attendants were moved to Ajanta, which had a more substantial *pettah* wall.

Wellesley marched for Ajanta on September 30 and down the Ghaut, which had a descent of three miles. The two British armies were again to remain separate, but would work closely together. Wellesley once more used Stevenson as his eyes and ears. Word soon reached Wellesley that Scindia and Berar had retreated to Burhampoor, threatening to raid south down towards Poona. Leaving Stevenson in the north with orders to take Burhampoor, Wellesley started to march in a westerly direction and then south with the intention of cutting off the Marathas if their plan to raid into the Peshwa's territories was to be believed. However, on October 6 whilst at Wakri he received information to the contrary. By October 8 he was back at Ajanta. Stevenson arrived outside Burhampoor on October 8 and after a short, sharp fight captured the town on October 16. Believing that Scindia and Berar once again threatened to move south, Wellesley moved in the same direction and was halfway to Aurangabad when on October 11 he received intelligence from his *hircarrahs* that Scindia and Berar had separated on September 29. Scindia had retired westwards and was intent on raiding into the Peshwa's and Nizam's territories, and Berar was heading north to Burhampoor, but was not in a fit state to challenge Stevenson.

THE CAPTURE OF ASSEERGHUR

The British army did not live off the land and so needed supply depots in order to operate freely. Wellesley had come to the conclusion that he

Dowlautabad Fort outside Aurangabad. Wellesley wanted his wounded to be cared for inside the fort's grounds, but was refused by the Nizam's *killadar*. The Nizam was very secretive about the fort's construction; outsiders were not allowed to approach within five miles of it. (Mary Evans Picture Library)

would need another base similar to Ahmednugger, but further north, if he was to chase down the Marathas. Asseerghur was the ideal place and consequently Stevenson was tasked with capturing the fortress at the earliest opportunity. His small army arrived outside Asseerghur on October 19 and Stevenson immediately set his men the task of constructing two siege batteries. His next move was to launch an attack on Asseerghur's *pettah*, which was taken relatively easily. Stevenson now offered terms to the fort's *killadar*, which were rejected. More British troops were deployed in the *pettah*, which in some places was only 150 yards from the fort. Stevenson was also urging on the completion of the siege battery positions, as there was the risk that the Maratha infantry might return and try to break the siege. The two siege battery positions were completed late on October 19; whereupon Stevenson sent word that the next day the batteries would commence firing. Stevenson hoped to avoid a costly assault in terms of casualties, and was still prepared to offer terms to the *killadar*, but the negotiations broke down on a couple of sticking points. The battery opened fire the next day, October 20, and after about one hour a white flag was seen to be flying; arrangements were made for the delivery of the hostages to Stevenson as per his terms. October 21 saw the garrison march out with their personal property, and it appears that the garrison accepted a bribe of 20,000 rupees to leave. The troops had not been paid and therefore Scindia was in breach of contract; so as far as the garrison was concerned they could surrender the fort with honour, for they had not let it fall, merely deciding not to fight when it became clear that the British

The fortress of Gwalighur was considered impregnable by the Marathas. It fell to Wellesley on December 15, 1803 and effectively ended Maratha resistance in the Deccan. (British Library/India Office)

would pay them. The capture of Asseerghur not only meant that the last of Scindia's strongholds in the Deccan had fallen, but that the British had gained the ability to control access between the Deccan and North India. With the capture of Burhampoor and Asseerghur also came the capture of ten of Scindia's European officers, who confirmed that Pohlmann's regular battalions had disbanded during the retreat after Assaye.

Wellesley moved north from Pahud on October 17 to be close to Stevenson's force, should Scindia and Berar re-unite, and on the 19th arrived at Ferdapoor. As it happened Berar did not try to save Asseerghur and actually marched between the two armies in a south-easterly direction on October 20, heading for the Nizam's territories. Wellesley, on learning of the move, immediately went back to Ajanta, arriving on October 25. The next day he wrote to Major Shaw:

Since the battle of Assaye I have been like a man who fights with one hand and defends himself with the other. With Colonel Stevenson's corps I have acted offensively, and have taken Asseerghur; and with my own, I have covered his operations, and defended the territories of the Nizam and the Peshwa. In doing this, I have made some terrible marches, but I have been remarkably fortunate, first, in stopping the enemy when they intended to pass to the southward, through the Casserbarry Ghaut; and afterwards, by a rapid march to the northward, in stopping Scindia when he was moving to interrupt Colonel Stevenson's operations against Asseerghur, in which he would otherwise undoubtedly have succeeded. I moved up the ghaut as soon as Colonel Stevenson got possession of Asseerghur; and I think that, in a day or two, I shall turn Ragojee Bhoonslah (Berar), who passed through to the southward. At all events I am in time to prevent him from

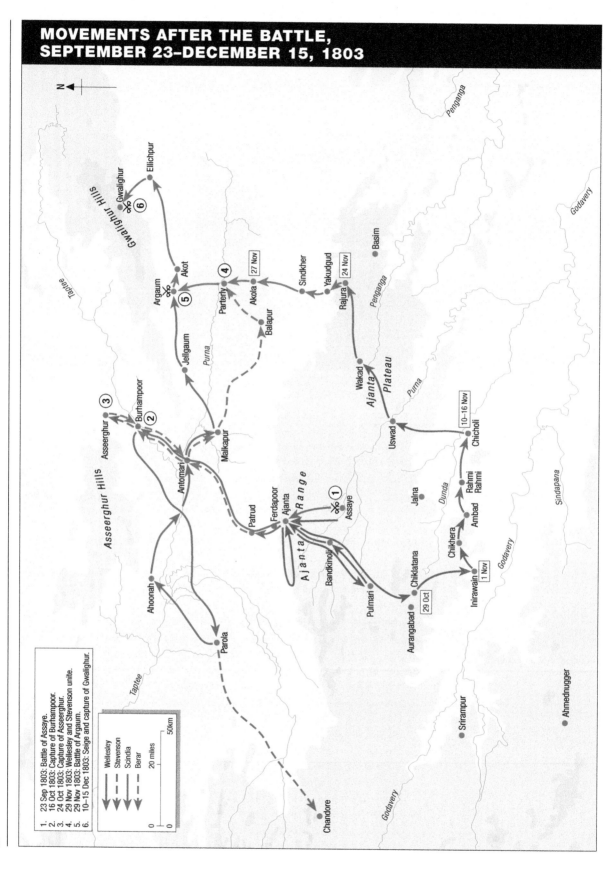

N

Penganga

Godavery

Ellichpur

Gwalighur ⑥

Gwalighur Hills

Akot

Argaum ⑤   Partenly ④   27 Nov   Akola   Sindkher   Yakudgud   24 Nov   Basim

Jellgaum   Balapur   Rajura   Penganga

Purna

Burhampoor ③   Wakad   Ajanta   Plateau

Asseerghur ②   Malkapur   Purna

Asseerghur Hills   Antomari

Patrud   Ferdapoor   Uswad   Chicholi   10–16 Nov

Purna   Ajanta ①   Assaye

Ahoonah   Bandkinoi   Ajanta Range   Jalna   Dunda   Rahmi Rahmi   Sindapana

Ambad

Chikhera

Parola   Pulmari   Chiklatana   Inirawain   1 Nov   Godavery

Aurangabad   29 Oct

Taptee

50km

Ahmednugger

Srirampur   Godavery

Chandore

1. 23 Sep 1803: Battle of Assaye.
2. 16 Oct 1803: Capture of Burhampoor.
3. 24 Oct 1803: Capture of Asseerghur.
4. 29 Nov 1803: Wellesley and Stevenson unite.
5. 29 Nov 1803: Battle of Argaum.
6. 10–15 Dec 1803: Seige and capture of Gwalighur.

Wellesley
Stevenson
Scindia
Berar

50km
20 miles
0   0

A Madras Native Infantry encampment below a fortress. (Author's collection)

doing any mischief. I think we are in great style to be able to act at all on the offensive in this quarter; but it is only done by the celerity of our movements, and by acting on the offensive or defensive with either corps, according to their situation and that of the enemy.

As if to illustrate his point his own 'corps', over the next eight days, put in extraordinary displays of marching, with upwards of 30 miles being covered each day as Wellesley chased down Berar and forced him to withdraw to his capital, in the north.

On November 10 Wellesley halted for a week at Chicholi, 15 miles north of the Godavery. He now directed Stevenson to prepare for a siege of Berar's fortress of Gwalighur and to watch out at the same time for Scindia. The next day Wellesley received in his camp representatives, *vakeels* (negotiators), from Scindia who was asking for an armistice. This did not come as a surprise to Wellesley, for by now he had received news of the successes of General Lake against Scindia's forces under General Perron in Hindustan. In a short period in August and September Lake had captured Alighur; won the Battle of Delhi on September 11; and occupied the old Mughal capital. An armistice with Scindia suited Wellesley, particularly if it meant that he could separate Berar from Scindia. This would enable him to take Gwalighur and move on to Berar's capital. However, the stipulation he gave to Scindia was that he had to remain 40 miles east of Ellichpur; Scindia would be too far away to help Berar, or to interfere with Poona or Hyderabad. Stevenson had started for Gwalighur on November 15, and on the 16th Wellesley began his own march northwards from Chicholi. On November 23 Scindia was granted an armistice, but did not take advantage of it and by remaining in the field an aura of distrust and suspicion fell over him. Wellesley's intelligence system was working exceptionally well at this time and his suspicions that Scindia's entreaties were to buy time were confirmed when he received news that Scindia was moving in the same direction as Berar.

In due course Scindia encamped at Sersooly, about four miles from an army commanded by Manoo Bapoo, in the service of the Raja of

The seal of Daulat Rao Scindia. (Author's collection)

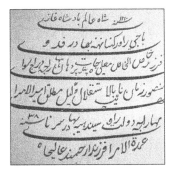

Berar. Clearly Scindia had not carried out the terms of the treaty that required him to be 20 *coss* (40 miles) east of Ellichpur, and when on November 28 his *vakeels* urgently pressed Wellesley not to attack Manoo Bapoo's troops, they were reminded that there was no suspension of arms with Berar and none with Scindia until he complied with the terms of the treaty. Wellesley also reminded them that he would continue to attack the enemies of the Company wherever he found them.

The next day, November 29, Wellesley and Stevenson united near the village of Parterly. They climbed to the top of a tower in the village and on looking through their telescopes they saw Bisnapah's Mysore cavalry, supported by the picquets of the day, skirmishing with the Maratha cavalry; beyond them, a line of infantry, artillery, and cavalry could be seen drawn up in a regular fashion on the plains of Argaum. Unfortunately, the events must be left for another book.

Maratha *pindarries* constantly raided British foraging parties and supply trains, which meant that all such activities required an escort. (Pen and ink by David Rowlands/private collection)

THE BATTLEFIELDS TODAY

I always try to visit a battlefield that I am to write about, as close as possible to the actual date that the battle was fought. With Assaye this was not possible, and (accompanied by my eldest son, Rupert) my visit took place in March 2005 when the temperatures were far hotter than they would have been in September.

We had a relatively short period of time available for the visit and so had to do as much as possible. To achieve this I decided we would start with Ahmadnagar (Ahmednugger) and then move on to Aurangabad, which would be our base for the visit to the battlefield. We arrived in Ahmadnagar by bus from Pune (Poona) and were initially hosted by the Indian Army MIRC, where Lieutenant-Colonel Sharnapa proved to be a very hospitable host. After our non-stop journey from the UK, the oasis of calm provided by the gardens of the officers' mess was a tonic. The next day our visit was to start in earnest.

The Bibi-Ka-Maqbara, the Mughal tomb-garden in Aurangabad. Completed in 1678 it was dedicated by Prince Azam Shah to his mother Begum Rabi'a Daurani, the great Mughal leader Aurangzeb's wife. (Rupert Millar)

Dowlautabad fort is a fascinating place to visit. It was one of the Nizam of Hyderabad's forts and its design was a closely guarded secret. (Author's photograph)

A wonderful view of the Deccan from only halfway up Dowlautabad Fort. (Author's photograph)

The map of Assaye on the wall of one of the houses in the village. (Author's photograph)

A little chap from Assaye, who tagged on to our battlefield tour, sits on a barrel in Peepalgaon. (Author's photograph)

Sadly I was unable to find any remnant of the *pettah* wall; I must admit that I did not have too much time to search in detail, but Ahmadnagar has changed dramatically over the years and so my quest might easily have been in vain anyway. The fortress, however, still stands and is just as imposing today. The fortress is the home of the Indian Army Armoured Corps, and so the first thing I did was to obtain permission from the adjutant to take photographs of the outside only. It is virtually impossible to identify where the breaching batteries were positioned, due to the military camps around the fort, but the fortifications are in remarkably good repair; Rupert and I agreed that Wellesley was lucky that the *killadar* did not offer more opposition, as the British did not really have a proper siege train, and so surely he could have frustrated Wellesley for longer? We walked around the outside of the fortress and came across two gun barrels mounted on bricks, both announcing the

fact that they had been used by the British in 1803 and that Wellesley had breakfasted nearby.

We went by taxi to Aurangabad, which enabled us to stop and look at things on the way. We stopped at Toka, on the Godavery River, which is close to where the British crossed. I was surprised at how wide the river was, and, as we were visiting India before the monsoon season, it was a shock to find as much water as we did in it; our driver, however, explained that the Godavery was very rarely a dry river course. The monsoon of 1803 is on record as being not particularly good, and I wonder if the water level that we saw was similar to that which confronted Wellesley. The river is wide and it is easy to see why it took a few days for the British army to cross.

Aurangabad is a bustling, noisy city with three gems to visit. A visit to the battlefield is not for the faint-hearted. Assaye itself is nearly 60 miles north-east of Aurangabad and will take nearly two hours to reach, with a lot of tooting of car horns and interesting overtaking decisions. By the time we had reached Assaye the temperature was 35°C – and the hard work was still to come! As soon as we arrived in the village, we were surrounded by a throng of very friendly and curious children and adults, who showed us a plan of the battle on a wall of one of the buildings; this is the first indication that you are in Assaye. We were very lucky that our driver, Gaikwa, was a Maratha, for the villagers do not speak Hindi but Marathi; thus, someone who speaks the language is essential.

The first site we were shown was the 'Englishman's grave'. The villagers believe adamantly that it dates from the battle. The grave is in the shade of a banyan tree and is very overgrown and surrounded by a low wall. If it is a grave from the battle, my guess is that it is of Colonel Maxwell; he was the senior British casualty at Assaye and the grave is in the right place for his

The Assaye colour of the 78th Foot (Rossshire Buffs). The three King's regiments were all granted permission to have an Assaye colour and to wear the elephant as a badge. (Author's photograph)

last charge. From here we decided to leave Gaikwa at Assaye and to walk to Pimpalgaon (Peepalgaon) and Varud (Waroor). This was a truly 'mad dogs and Englishmen' decision! Jac Weller says that there was more vegetation when he was writing (1968) than in 1803. I do not know if this is true, but the land is still farmed pretty much as it was in 1803, with cereal crops and onion fields predominating. I saw one tractor, but otherwise it was oxen and plough. There are a lot of trees scattered about the area, but again I think this is as it was at the time. We started our walk from the Maratha position, and the Maratha artillery must have been firing at the dust clouds raised by the British infantry as they approached the Kailna; for Pimpalgaon can just be seen, but not the ford. There was not a drop of water in the Kailna when we visited; it is, however, easy to imagine that in a good monsoon season the waters would be 10ft deep and therefore only crossable at the fords. Diarists, such as Blakiston, record that the water was three feet at the ford. After crossing over the ford we went and stood at the 550m height spot, which is approximately half way to the ford over the Juah River near Borkerry and is also in the centre of the ground covered by Wellesley's army. Looking west the ground rises very gently towards the Maratha line, where it is only five metres higher. The walk westwards towards the Maratha line leaves a clear impression that, although there is the odd fold in the ground, Wellesley's infantry were exposed most of the time to the Maratha artillery fire during their advance. Assaye village itself has lost most of the walls that encased the village at the time, and even when Jac Weller visited in the 1960s. Today there is only the occasional short stretch, which is disappointing.

There is not a lot to see, but visiting the field of Assaye under the intense Indian sun makes one realize how tough it was to be a soldier, particularly a European soldier, in India in 1803 and for this alone, the visit is worthwhile.

BIBLIOGRAPHY AND FURTHER READING

The following list is a selection of books for those readers who may wish to delve more deeply into this fascinating period of British colonial history. I can particularly recommend Blakiston, Welsh, Pester, and Thorn, as they fought in the Maratha campaigns of 1803 – what more can be said?

Bayley, C.A., *Empire and Information: Intelligence Gathering and Social Communication in India, 1780–1870,* Cambridge University Press, 1996

Blakiston, Capt J., *Twelve Years' Military Adventure in Three Quarters of the Globe,* 2 vols, London, 1829

Biddulph, Col John, *The Nineteenth and Their Times, being an Account of the Four Cavalry Regiments in the British Army that Have borne the number Nineteen and the Campaigns in which they served,* London, 1899

Burton, Maj R.G., *Wellington's Campaigns in India,* Calcutta 1908, (Reprint San Diego) 1997

Compton, Herbert, *A Particular Account of the European Military Adventurers of Hindoostan from 1784 to 1803,* London, 1892

Cooper, Randolf, *The Anglo Maratha Campaigns and the Contest for India,* Cambridge University Press, 2003

Davidson, Maj H., *History and Services of the 78th Highlanders (Ross-shire Buffs),* 2 vols, Edinburgh, 1901

Duff, James Grant, *A History of the Marathas,* 3 vols, London, 1826

Forbes, James, *Oriental Memoirs,* 2 vols, London, 1834

Fortescue, The Hon. John, *A History of the British Army,* 13 vols, vol V, London, 1921

Fortescue, The Hon. John, *Wellington,* London, 1925

Gleig, Rev G.R., *Life of Arthur, Duke of Wellington,* London, 1871

Gordon, Stewart, *The New Cambridge History of India II.4, The Marathas, 1600–1818,* Cambridge University Press, 1993

Gurwood, Lt Col, *The Dispatches of Field Marshal The Duke of Wellington,* 8 vols, vol 1 India and 2 India, London, 1852

Khanna, D.D., *Battle of Assaye 1803,* University of Allahabad, 1981

Malleson, Col G.B., *The Decisive Battles of India from 1746 to 1849,* London, (reprint) 1914

Mason, Phillip, *A Matter of Honour, An Account of the Indian Army its Officers and Men,* London, 1974

Pearce, Robert, *Memoirs and Correspondence of the Most Noble Richard, Marquess Wellesley,* 3 vols, London, 1846

Pester, Lt John, *War and Sport in India 1802–1806, an Officer's Diary,* London, 1912

Pitre, Brig K.G., *Second Anglo–Maratha War 1802–1805: a Study in Military History,* Poona, 1990

Roberts, Gen Lord, VC, *The Rise of Wellington,* London, 1895

Roberts, P. E., *India under Wellesley,* Allahabad, (Reprint) 1961

Sardesai, Govind S., *New History of the Marathas,* Bombay, (Reprint) 1968

Sen, Surendra Nath, *The Military System of the Marathas,* New Delhi, (Reprint) 1979

Sen, S.P., *The French in India,* New Delhi, 1958

Thorn, Maj William, *Memoir of the War in India Conducted by General Lord Lake, Commander in Chief and Major-General Sir Arthur Wellesley, Duke of Wellington; from its Commencement in 1803, to its Termination in 1806, on the Banks of the Hyphasis,* London, 1818

Weller, Jac, *Wellington in India,* London, 1972

Wellington, the Second Duke of (ed), *Supplementary Dispatches and Memoranda of Field Marshal Arthur Duke of Wellington, K.G,* 15 vols, London, 1859

Welsh, Col James, *Military Reminiscences,* 2 vols, London, 1830

INDEX